WEEKEND MAKES

PATCHWORK

25 QUICK AND EASY PROJECTS TO MAKE

WEEKEND MAKES

PATCHWORK

25 QUICK AND EASY PROJECTS TO MAKE

JANET GODDARD

First published 2019 by
Guild of Master Craftsman Publications Ltd Castle Place,
166 High Street, Lewes,
East Sussex, BN7 1XU

Print ISBN 978 1 78494 511 4

A catalogue record for this book is available from the
British Library.

Senior Project Editor: Elizabeth Betts
Managing Art Editor: Darren Brant
Art Editor: Lindsay Birch
Photographer: Jesse Wild
Stylist: Jaine Bevan

Colour origination by GMC Reprographics
Printed and bound in China

CONTENTS

INTRODUCTION

Welcome to *Weekend Makes - Patchwork*, a book featuring twenty-five fresh, bright and modern projects to make for yourself, your home or to give as gifts.

Life can be busy, and often we don't always have the time to be able to commit to larger or more difficult projects as they are just too time-consuming. However, the patchwork projects in this book can all be easily completed in a weekend. Some of the projects are super quick and can be stitched in just an hour, while others will take a few hours or a day. The projects are graded as 'Easy' or 'Requires Experience'. Basic sewing skills are needed for the 'Easy' projects and they are suitable for beginners. The 'Requires Experience' projects involve a few more steps and will take a little longer to make.

I love working with fabric and have enjoyed using a wide range of colours and prints to make the projects. These include highly patterned designs, quieter plains and more minimalistic modern prints. The combination of fabrics emphasises the geometric shapes created by the patchwork so, when choosing your fabrics, place them together to see how they look. Each pattern includes sewing instructions, step by step photos, information for quilting as well as a few tips. To speed up, and therefore simplify the process, there are no pattern pieces and all you will need is a rotary cutting set.

The projects are all stitched on the sewing machine with sometimes a little hand stitching to finish, such as attaching buttons or bindings. Where quilted, this is done using a domestic sewing machine with simple straight line or wavy quilting.

A section on patchwork techniques can be found at the front of the book and I suggest that you read this first before beginning. It provides a really good starting point and describes all the basics in detail.

The twenty-five projects in this book are stylish but also practical for everyday use. I have so enjoyed designing and making them and hope that you will enjoy stitching them too.

Janet Goddard

EQUIPMENT

Good quality basic equipment is needed. There is no need to spend a fortune on the latest gadgets, just invest in some good quality essential resources.

Sewing machine: The most important piece of equipment for patchwork and quilting is a sewing machine. It really only needs to be able to stitch forwards and backwards and doesn't need a whole lot of fancy stitches although a zigzag stitch can be handy for neatening seams. It is important that your machine is cared for and is cleaned and serviced regularly to keep it working well. A little oil applied, according to the manufacturer's instructions, should help to keep everything in good order. Changing the needle regularly also helps with the quality of stitching, so I usually change the needle on the machine every time I begin a new project. The machine feet used the most are the ¼in (0.65cm) patchwork foot which is excellent for maintaining ¼in (0.65cm) wide seams, the zipper foot for stitching in zips and the walking foot used for machine quilting.

Rotary cutter, ruler and mat: All the pieces for the quilt projects in this book can be cut on a rotary cutting mat (1) using a rotary cutter (2) and a ruler (3).

A rotary cutting mat is a self-healing mat designed to be used with a rotary cutter. Mats come with grid markings on them which can be used with the ruler for accurate cutting. If you are purchasing a mat for the first time buy the largest you can afford. A 24 x 36in (61 x 91.5cm) mat is a good investment.

A rotary cutter is a cutting instrument with a round-wheeled blade. This is used with an acrylic ruler and a self-healing cutting mat. A good quality rotary cutter should have a protective safety shield on it that can be pushed on and off. It is important to train yourself to always make sure that the safety cover is on the blade every time the cutter is put down. Blades are sharp and can cut through up to eight layers of fabric at a time and so can do a lot of damage to hands if not kept safe. Replace the blade when it starts to become blunt.

Rulers come in many shapes and sizes, are marked in inches or centimetres and are made of tough acrylic. I personally find the rulers with yellow markings the easiest to see on fabric but this is a personal choice. If you are purchasing just one ruler make it a 6 × 24in (15 × 61cm) ruler as this can be used for most projects.

Scissors: A good sharp pair of dressmaking scissors **(4)** is essential for tasks such as cutting through wadding (batting). A medium size pair **(5)** is useful for cutting off corners and trimming, while a small pair **(6)** is handy for snipping threads.

Pins: I use flat flower head fine pins **(7)** for patchwork as they help to keep the fabric flat, but any type of pins will do.

Needles: Hand sewing needles are used for some finishing off techniques and are available in many sizes. Sharps are good for general sewing and hand stitching binding.

Clips: (8 and 9) These are great for holding multiple layers together when hand stitching a binding to a project or topstitching around the top of a bag. The clips are plastic (think mini clothes pegs but better) and can be removed easily as you stitch.

Fabric markers: There are many fabric markers **(10)** available but any marker should be easy to use, easy to see and simple to remove after you have finished sewing. Markers are used to mark measurements for cutting or stitching and also quilting lines or patterns. Several different markers are needed in order to contrast with both light and dark fabrics. White and silver markers, water-erasable pens and chalk markers are all useful.

Seam ripper: (11) This is often called a 'quick unpick' and usually comes as a tool with the sewing machine. Hugely useful for removing tacking (basting) stitches or the odd mistake we all make now and then.

Safety pins: (12) These are really useful for holding the layers together when quilting.

Thread: (13) A selection of pale grey, dark grey and beige threads are the most useful colours for piecing.

Iron and ironing board: After the sewing machine the iron is the most useful tool for patchwork. A press with a dry iron is all that is needed and the use of a good quality iron does make a difference to the finished product. The ironing surface needs to be firm and clean.

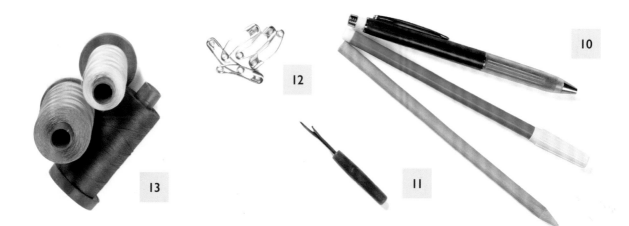

MEASUREMENTS

All the cutting instructions for the projects include a ¼in (0.65cm) seam allowance. I have used imperial as the standard measurement throughout all my patterns, but the metric measurements have been included as well. Use either imperial or metric, and do not mix the two together.

FABRIC AND THREAD

One of the nicest parts of starting a new project is being able to choose the fabrics. I have made fabric choices to suit the project design. If the patchwork uses large shapes I have tended to use fabric that has a larger scale print design, and for smaller shapes the fabric print has tended to be smaller as well. Many of the projects use small amounts of fabric which I have been able to source from my scrap box.

All of the projects in this book use fabric that is 100 per cent cotton and of a high-quality. If different fabric weights are used together it can adversely affect the overall quality and strength of the finished item.

The fabric allowances in the patterns are for fabric that is approximately 42in wide (107cm) from selvedge to selvedge. I always cut the selvedge from the fabric before beginning a project and rarely pre-wash fabrics, but this is a personal choice.

The fabric allowances in each pattern allow for approximately 2-3in (5-7.5cm) extra so if a small mistake is made you shouldn't run out of fabric, however, do try to be as careful as possible.

The best thread for patchwork is high quality cotton thread. I tend to use a 50-weight grey thread for general piecing. For quilting I use a 40-weight thread in a colour that complements or contrasts with the fabric.

ROTARY CUTTING

Most of the fabric pieces for the patterns in this book can be cut using a rotary cutter. If you are new to using a rotary cutter it is worth spending some time practising on scrap fabric, as accuracy does improve with practice.

1 To cut safely, always hold the cutter firmly in your hand at a 45 degree angle and place your other hand on the ruler. The hand on the ruler needs to be flat with the fingers slightly opened, making sure that your fingers are away from the edges of the ruler. Flip the safety cover off the cutter and place the blade next to the ruler. Starting at the bottom of the fabric, begin to cut away from yourself until you have cut past the end of the fabric.

Close the safety cover on the cutter before putting the cutter down. It is easier to stand and cut rather than sit, and a kitchen work surface is usually at an appropriate height.

The patchwork shapes in this book consist of squares, rectangles and triangles. All of these can be cut from strips of fabric that have been cut to specific widths.

Before you make your first cut, iron the fabric to remove any wrinkles.

2 Fold the fabric selvedge to selvedge. If you use a 24in (61cm) long ruler you should not need to fold the fabric again but if your ruler is shorter you may need to fold the fabric again so that the fold is on the selvedge. Ensure that all the layers are smooth. Place the ruler firmly on top of the fabric and cut the selvedge from the fabric, tidying up any uneven edges.

To cut strips of fabric from which further shapes can be cut, align the even horizontal edge of the fabric with the first vertical measurement on the cutting board.

3 Place the ruler on top so that the measurement you wish to cut is in line with the edge of the fabric, for example if you wish to cut a 2in (5cm) strip the 2in (5cm) marking of the ruler will be level with the cut edge of the fabric. Line up the cutter with the ruler and cut away from yourself.

It is then easy to cut the strips into shapes for the patchwork pieces.

4 If you wish to cut squares, place the strip on the cutting board horizontally and then, using the ruler vertically, measure the same width as the strip, keeping a ruler line on the long edge of the strip, ensuring that a right angle is maintained and that you are cross cutting the strip into squares. Rectangles can be cut in a similar manner.

5 To cut right-angled triangles, cut squares as described above, and then cut the squares in half on the diagonal from corner to corner. Make sure that you hold the ruler firmly when cutting on the diagonal as it is easy to wobble and then the triangles will not be consistent in size.

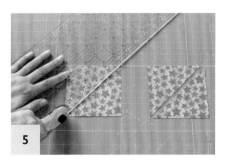

PATCHWORK TECHNIQUES

The patchwork techniques used in the projects in this book feature squares, rectangles, right-angled triangles, flying geese units or strips. All of the patchwork and general construction is stitched on the sewing machine however in some projects there is some hand finishing. The hand finishing may involve stitching on a button, slip stitching an opening closed or sewing down the underside of the binding. Each pattern explains how to stitch the shapes together and has photos to show the stages, but the patchwork process is explained in more detail below:

Basic piecing techniques

Basic piecing involves stitching two shapes together using a standard straight stitch on the machine. The raw edges of the shapes must be aligned precisely in order for the patchwork to be accurate. When piecing patchwork you do not need to back stitch at the beginning and end of a seam, as often the next seam will cross over it. All seams are ¼in (0.65cm) wide. **(1)**

If you have a patchwork foot on your sewing machine you can align the edge of the foot with the edge of the fabric to get an accurate seam. If you do not have a patchwork foot you can adjust the needle position so that an accurate seam is achieved.

To chain piece squares and rectangles

If you have lots of squares or rectangles to stitch together you can chain piece them. Place the first two shapes right sides together, making sure that the edges to be stitched line up. Using the patchwork foot on the machine, line up the edge of the fabric with the edge of the foot. Stitch along the seam line, but when you reach the end of the fabric leave the needle down, lift the presser foot and slip the next two pieces to be stitched under the foot, leaving a small space between it and the previously stitched fabric. Continue stitching in this way to make a chain of patchwork shapes. It looks just like patchwork bunting. Once you

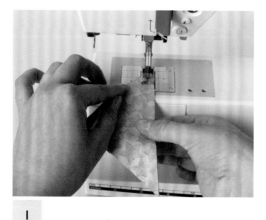

1

2

3

have stitched the pieces, cut them apart and continue to join the shapes together as needed.

To piece right-angled triangles

These triangles are often called half-square triangles. They are pieced by starting with squares. To stitch two triangles start with two squares, each in a different fabric. Draw a line on the diagonal, on the wrong side of one of the squares. Place the squares on top of each other with right sides facing and the edges aligned. **(2)**

Stitch ¼in (0.65cm) on each side of the drawn diagonal line. Cut apart on the diagonal line **(3)**, press seams towards the darker fabric. **(4 and 5)**

To piece flying geese units

This method of stitching triangles is fast and also avoids having to stitch on a cut bias edge. However, it does waste fabric as you are cutting off and discarding excess fabric. To make one flying geese unit you will need a rectangle and two squares cut to the appropriate measurement. Draw a line on the diagonal on the wrong side of each square. Position a square on one side of the rectangle, right sides facing, so that the drawn diagonal line travels from the bottom corner to the middle of the rectangle. **(6)**

Stitch on the drawn line. Trim away the excess fabric ¼in (0.65cm) from the stitching. **(7)** Fold the triangle back and press. **(8)** Repeat on the other side of the rectangle. **(9)**

4

5

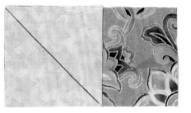
6

7

8

9

This is a quick way to make four flying geese units at a time. It starts with one large square in one fabric and four smaller squares in a second fabric. Draw a line on the diagonal on the wrong side of all the small squares. Position two small squares on diagonally opposite corners of the large square, so that the drawn line is running from corner to corner, and stitch ¼in (0.65cm) away from each side of the drawn line. **(10)**

Cut along the drawn line **(11)** and press seams towards the small triangles. **(12)**
Position the final two squares on the remaining unstitched corners of each unit so that the diagonal line is positioned between the two smaller triangles. Stitch a ¼in (0.65cm) seam away from each side of the drawn line. **(13)**
Cut along the drawn line **(14 and 15)** and press seams towards the small triangles. This produces four flying geese units. **(16 and 17)**

To match intersections

It is important that seams match and points are sharp when piecing. When seams meet at an intersection make sure that the seam allowances are pressed in opposite directions. The seam allowances should butt together and can be pinned through the stitching lines to hold the pieces in place before stitching. This same principle can be used when diagonal seams need to meet when stitching triangles to one another. I usually pin the patchwork shapes together by putting the pins in vertically to the stitching line rather than horizontally. The pins can then be removed just before the needle of the machine reaches the pin.

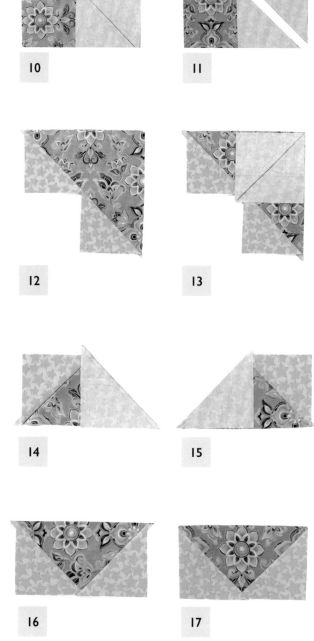

10 11
12 13
14 15
16 17

Preparation for quilting

To get your project ready for quilting, first press the patchwork top and backing fabric to ensure that there are no creases. On a large flat space, such as the floor or a table, lay out the backing fabric with the right side facing downwards. Then lay the wadding (batting) on top, smoothing out any wrinkles. Finally, place the patchwork on top, right side facing upwards in the centre. There will be excess backing fabric and wadding (batting) around each side. Smooth the top until it is flat, with no bumps or creases. Then, starting in the centre of the top, pin or tack (baste) the layers together. Work methodically, in a grid format, securing the layers at 10cm (4in) intervals.

Many of the smaller projects and bags use fusible wadding (batting). This is pre-treated with a heat activated adhesive so when it is ironed to the wrong side of the fabric it does not move or shift around which means no pinning is required. It is always important to follow the manufacturer's instructions when using fusible wadding (batting) as the heat setting and amount of time it takes to fuse can vary.

Quilting

All the projects in this book have been machine quilted with simple straight or wavy lines, and each pattern mentions the design I have used. Using a walking foot helps to make the quilting easier as the layers are fed through the machine evenly. However, if you do not have a walking foot you can use an ordinary presser foot but make sure to reduce both the thread tension and foot pressure on the machine to prevent the layers from puckering. It can help to make a sample square from scrap fabric and wadding (batting) and test the settings before starting on your project. I use the same thread in the top and bobbin of my machine and like to use a 40-weight thread which is strong, but fine enough to sink into the quilt layers to create texture. Increase the stitch length before beginning; my preference is to a setting of 3mm (⅛in).

Binding

When choosing the fabric for the binding you can either choose a fabric that is already in the project which will help pull the colours together or choose a new fabric that complements the project. The quilts, placemats and table runner in this book have all been bound with a double fold binding.

To bind the project, trim the excess backing and wadding (batting) level with the edge of the patchwork top. It should be square, if not use your ruler and rotary cutter to square it up. Stitch the binding strips together to form one continuous strip; this can either be on the straight or at a 45-degree angle. Press seams open to reduce bulk. Fold the strip in half lengthways, wrong sides together, and press. Starting at the top on one side, match the raw edges of the binding to the raw edge of the project and sew in place. Repeat on the other side of the project and then the top and bottom. Finally, fold the binding over to the back of the item and neatly slip stitch in place by hand.

If a project has curved edges it needs to be bound with bias binding, and this will be stated in the pattern instructions. To cut bias strips from fabric, fold the fabric on the diagonal to make a triangle. Cut the strips to the required width across the diagonal starting at the folded edge. The larger the folded triangle the longer the bias strip. Strips can be stitched together to get the required length.

PIN CUSHION

A pin cushion is an essential piece of equipment for anyone who sews. This version is large enough to store lots of pins, but stylish enough to leave out on display. A great project to use up tiny pieces of special fabric that you have been saving, it can easily be finished within an hour.

SKILL LEVEL: EASY

YOU'LL NEED:

FABRIC

Requirements based on fabrics with a useable width of 107cm (42in):

- 10in (25.4cm) peach print for the outer pin cushion

- Six 2in (5cm) squares of a variety of printed fabrics for the patchwork

HABERDASHERY

- Neutral thread for piecing
- Polyester toy filling
- Large button for decoration

Tip

I have stuffed my pin cushion with polyester toy filling, but if you prefer you can buy a special stuffing for pin cushions which is heavier and helps to keep the pins sharp.

If you wish to add an alternative decoration to the pin cushion try stitching some lace or ric rac to the front instead of the button.

PIN CUSHION

Size: 4½ × 9½in (11.5 × 24cm)

PREPARATION:

The pin cushion is made up of six squares and a rectangle. It is embellished with a large decorative button.

CUTTING

All cutting instructions include a ¼in (0.65cm) seam allowance.

Peach print fabric

*   One 6½ × 5in (16.5 × 12.7cm) rectangle
*   One 9½ × 5in (24 × 12.7cm) rectangle

Printed fabrics

From each of the six printed fabrics cut:

*   One 2in (5cm) square

METHOD

To stitch the patchwork:

1 Place the six 2in (5cm) printed fabric squares into pairs with right sides together and stitch. Press seams to one side. Stitch the pairs together to make a grid two squares by three squares. Press seams downwards.

2 Sew the 6½ × 5in (16.5 × 12.7cm) peach print rectangle to the side of the unit completed in Step 1. Press the seam away from the patchwork.

To finish the pin cushion:

3 With right sides together, place the unit completed in Step 2 on top of the 9½ × 5in (24 × 12.7cm) peach print rectangle and sew around each side, leaving a 2in (5cm) gap in stitching in the middle of one of the long sides. Trim the corners and turn the pin cushion through the gap so it is right side out. Stuff with the polyester toy filling, pushing it in firmly, then close the opening with small, neat slip stitches.

4 Sew the large button to one corner, stitching through all the layers.

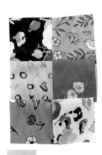

1

2

3

4

NEEDLE CASE

Protect and store your needles in a sweet handmade needle case. This is a great project to use up tiny pieces of special fabric and particularly useful for taking sewing projects out and about. Team the needle case with the pin cushion for a sweet gift for a sewing friend.

SKILL LEVEL: EASY

YOU'LL NEED:

FABRIC

Requirements based on fabrics with a useable width of 107cm (42in):

- 5in (12.7cm) peach print for the outer and inner needle case

- Nine 2in (5cm) squares of printed fabrics for the patchwork

WADDING (BATTING)

- 9½ x 5in (24 x 12.7cm) fusible wadding (batting)

HABERDASHERY

- Neutral thread for piecing

- 12in (30.5cm) length of beige ribbon, ⅛in (0.32cm) wide

- 8 x 3½in (20.3 x 8.9cm) blue felt for the inside

- One small button

Tips

When you get to Step 3, tuck the ribbons in towards the middle of the book so they do not get caught in the seam.

If you wish to add a further page to your needle case sew in a second piece of felt then you get to Step 4.

NEEDLE CASE

Size: 4½ × 9½in (11.5 × 24cm)

PREPARATION:

The outer needle case is constructed with a nine patch on the front and plain fabric on the back, while the inside contains a felt insert for storing needles and pins. It is finished with a ribbon and button tie.

CUTTING

All cutting instructions include a ¼in (0.65cm) seam allowance.

Peach print fabric

- One 9½ × 5in (24 × 12.7cm) rectangle
- One 5in (12.7cm) square

Printed fabrics

From each of the nine printed fabrics cut:

- One 2in (5cm) square

Fusible wadding (batting)

- One 9½ × 5in (24 × 12.7cm) rectangle

Blue felt

- One 8 × 3½in (20.3 × 8.9cm) rectangle

METHOD

To stitch the patchwork:

1 Place the nine 2in (5cm) printed fabric squares in a three by three grid. With right sides together stitch the squares into three rows. Press the seams in each row in alternate directions. Stitch the rows together and press seams downwards.

2 Stitch the 5in (12.7cm) peach print square to the side of the unit completed in Step 2. Press the seam away from the patchwork.

To finish the needle case:

3 Iron the fusible wadding (batting) to the wrong side of the pieced unit completed in Step 2. Place it on a surface with the right side facing up, then fold the ribbon in half and pin the folded end in the middle of the side at the opposite end to the patchwork. Stitch it in place $\frac{1}{8}$in (0.32cm) from the edge. Then, with right sides together, place the pieced unit on top of the 9½ x 5in (24 x 12.7cm) peach print rectangle and stitch around each side, leaving a 2in (5cm) gap in stitching in the middle of one of the long sides. Trim the corners and turn the needle case through the gap so it is right side out and push out the corners. Close the opening with small, neat slip stitches.

4 Lay the 8 x 3½in (20.3 x 8.9cm) felt rectangle on the inside of the needle case and pin it in the centre. Sew a single line of stitching down through the centre. This should line up with the seam in the centre of the front.

5 Stitch the button to the front of the case, ensuring that it aligns with the ribbon. To close, bring the ribbon around to the front and tie in a bow.

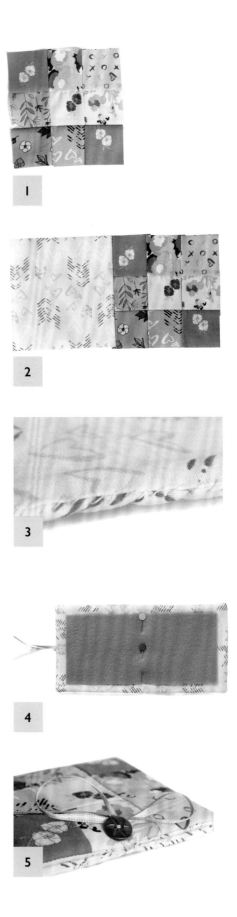

PRETTY POUCHES

A speedy afternoon make that is perfect for storing cosmetics, toiletries, stationery or sewing supplies. You can match the zip to the fabrics as I have done or choose a different coloured zip for a contrast effect. There are two designs to choose from, or you could make one of each!

SKILL LEVEL: REQUIRES EXPERIENCE

YOU'LL NEED:

FABRIC

Requirements based on fabrics with a useable width of 107cm (42in):

- 10in (25.4cm) pink spot for the outer pouch

- 2in (5cm) beige print for the patchwork

- 2in (5cm) pink floral for the patchwork

- 10in (25.4cm) floral print for the lining

WADDING (BATTING)

10in (15.4cm) fusible wadding (batting)

HABERDASHERY

- Pink thread

- One 8in (20.3cm) pink zip

- 4in (10cm) of ribbon, ⅛in (0.3cm) wide

PRETTY POUCHES

Size: 8½ x 7 x 2½in (21.6 x 17.8 x 6.3cm)

PREPARATION:

There are two versions to make, squares or strips, both of which are double sided. This project would suit fabrics with a smaller print and is ideal for using up small scraps.

Tip

It is very important that the zip is opened halfway in Step 7. If you forget, then you are unable to turn your pouch out to the right side.

CUTTING

All cutting instructions include a ¼in (0.65cm) seam allowance.

Pink spot fabric

*   Two 9 x 3in (23 x 7.5cm) rectangles
*   Two 9 x 4½in (23 x 11.5cm) rectangles

Beige print fabric

*   Six 2in (5cm) squares

Pink floral fabric

*   Six 2in (5cm) squares

Floral print fabric

*   Two 9 x 8½in (23 x 21.6cm) rectangles

Fusible wadding (batting)

*   Two 9 x 8½in (23 x 21.6cm) rectangles

METHOD

To stitch the outer pouch:

1 Take the six beige print and six pink floral 2in (5cm) squares and stitch them together into two rows of six squares, alternating the fabrics. Press the seams in each row in one direction. Trim ¼in (0.65cm) from the end of each row so it is 9in (23cm) long.

2 Stitch a 9 x 3in (23 x 7.5cm) pink spot rectangle to the top of each unit completed in Step 1 and a 9 x 4½in (23 x 11.5cm) pink spot rectangle to the bottom. Press seams towards the pink spot fabric.

3 Iron the fusible wadding (batting) to the wrong side of each of the units completed in Step 2.

4 Quilt vertical lines from top to bottom through both the fabric and wadding (batting) at 1½in (4cm) intervals across each outer pouch section.

5 To attach the zip, place the first outer pouch section right side up and place the zip face down on front of it, matching the top edge. Place a 9 x 8½in (23 x 21.6cm) rectangle of floral print fabric on top, right side down, and stitch along the top edge to secure the lining, zip and outer pouch.

6 Repeat Step 5 to attach the zip to the second pouch section, then open out each panel and press. Stitch ¼in (0.65cm) each side of the zip.

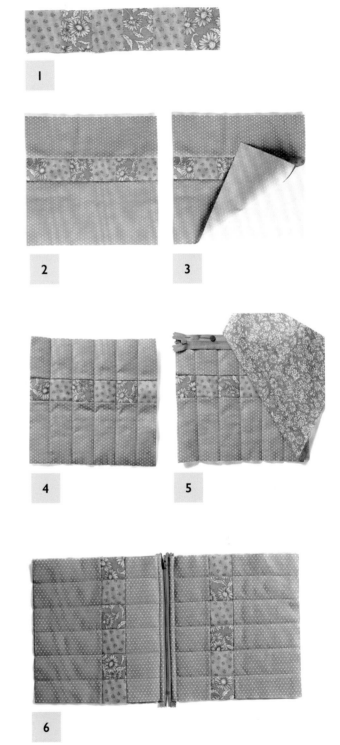

To stitch the pouch together:

7 Open the zip halfway and place the two outer pouch sections right sides together, and also the lining panels right sides together. Pin and stitch all the way around the edge, leaving a 3in (7.5cm) gap in stitching in the bottom of the lining.

8 To shape the base match the centre fold of the base with the side seam. Measure in 2¼in (5.7cm) along the seam line and stitch across. Cut off the excess fabric. Repeat on the other corner, and then on both corners of the lining. Turn the pouch through the opening in the lining so it is right side out. Stitch the opening closed. To finish, tie the ribbon to the zip pull.

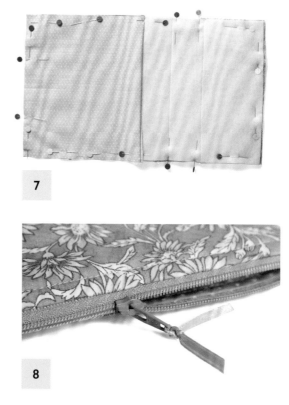

7

8

STRIP POUCH YOU'LL NEED:

. . . .

To make the strip version substitute the 2in (5cm) squares for two 9 x 2in (23 x 5cm) strips of beige fabric. Follow the instructions from Step 2, quilting horizontal lines ¼in (0.65cm) from the seam line.

Tip

When stitching the outer sections and lining panels together it does make a difference if the teeth of the zip point towards the lining fabric. This makes the part of the pouch where the zip meets the side seam look much neater.

FLORAL APRON

This apron is ever so practical, and the addition of the patchwork detail makes it a very stylish addition to your home. Whether you are cooking, gardening or working on DIY projects, the deep patchwork pocket is a handy feature. The use of shop-bought tape for the ties helps to speed up the sewing time.

SKILL LEVEL: EASY

YOU'LL NEED:

FABRIC

Requirements based on fabrics with a useable width of 107cm (42in):

- 40in (1m) red floral fabric for the apron

- 6in (15.2cm) green floral for the patchwork and pocket borders

- 12in (30cm) cream floral for the patchwork and pocket lining

HABERDASHERY

- 72in (183cm) red tape for the ties, ½in (1.3cm) wide

- Neutral thread for piecing the patchwork

- Red thread for stitching the apron

- Marking pencil

FLORAL APRON

Size: 24½ × 32½in (62.3 × 80cm)

PREPARATION:

The patchwork pocket is made from fifteen small squares, which are bordered and then sewn to the apron.

Tip

To divide the pocket into two smaller sections topstitch down the middle of the pocket when sewing it to the apron

I have used 100% cotton fabric for my apron, but if you prefer you could use a heavier weight fabric such as a cotton drill.

CUTTING

All cutting instructions include a ¼in (0.65cm) seam allowance.

Red fabric

- One 26 × 34in (66 × 86cm) rectangle

Green fabric

- Eight 2½in (6.3cm) squares
- Four 2½ × 10½in (6.3 × 26.5cm) strips

Cream fabric

- Seven 2½in (6.3cm) squares
- One 10½ × 14½in (26.5 × 37cm) rectangle

Red tape

- One 22in (56cm) length
- Two 25in (63.5cm) lengths

METHOD

To stitch the apron

1 To form the apron shape take the 26 × 34in (66 × 86cm) red rectangle and fold it in half lengthways. Measure 23in (58.4cm) up from the bottom along the raw edge and make a mark. Along the top edge measure 6in (15.2cm) in from the fold and make a mark. To create the diagonal shaping draw a line between these two marks and cut. Unfold the apron.

2 To create a hem, fold and press under ¼in (0.65cm) on both straight sides of the apron. Then turn over ½in (1.3cm), press, then stitch with the red thread. Repeat across the bottom of the apron.

3 Take the two 25in (63.5cm) lengths of red tape and fold and stitch a hem on one end on each piece. Repeat Step 2 for the diagonal sections of the apron but, before stitching, slip the raw end of each piece of tape into the corner seam on each side where the diagonal meets the straight side. This will secure it in the stitching.

4 To stitch the top of the apron repeat Step 2 but, before stitching, slip the raw ends of the 22in (56cm) length of red tape into the corner seam where the diagonal meets the apron top so the tape forms a loop.

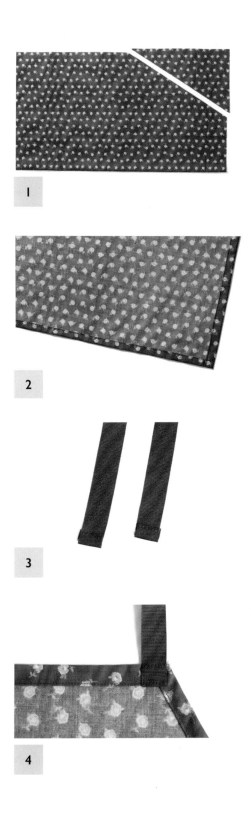

To stitch the patchwork pocket:

5 Take the fifteen 2½in (6.3cm) green and cream squares and lay them out into three rows of five squares, alternating the fabrics. Stitch the squares together in horizontal rows. Press seams in each row in opposite directions. Stitch the rows together and press seams downwards.

6 Stitch a 2½ × 10½in (6.3 × 26.5cm) green strip to the top and bottom of the patchwork. Press seams towards the strip. Then stitch a 2½ × 10½in (6.3 × 26.5cm) green strip to each side of the patchwork. Press seams towards the strip.

7 With right sides together, place the unit completed in Step 6 on top of the 10½ × 14½in (26.5 × 37cm) cream rectangle and stitch around each side, leaving a 4in (10cm) gap in stitching in the middle of one side. Trim the corners, turn through the gap and press.

To finish the apron:

8 To position the pocket on the apron front, measure 8in (20.3cm) up from the bottom and place the pocket centrally on top of the apron. Pin in place. Topstitch down each side and across the bottom ⅛in (0.32cm) in from the edge.

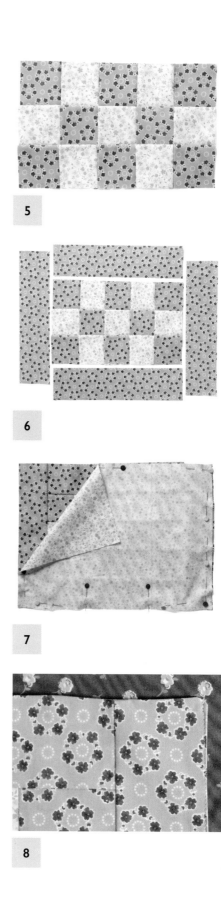

POT HOLDER

A pot holder is handy to have in the kitchen and this bright and cheerful one will help to make cooking a joy! This project is great for using up scraps and is sewn together using the quilt-as-you-go method which combines the piecing and quilting in the same process.

SKILL LEVEL: REQUIRES EXPERIENCE

YOU'LL NEED:

FABRIC

Requirements based on fabrics with a useable width of 107cm (42in):

- 15in (38cm) red floral fabric for the strips, backing, hanging loop and bias binding

- 3in (7.5cm) green floral fabric for the strips

- 3in (7.5cm) cream floral fabric for the strips

WADDING (BATTING)

- 10½ x 12½in (26.5 x 31.7cm) insulated wadding (batting)

HABERDASHERY

- Red thread for piecing

- Seam roller (optional)

- Marking pencil

> **Tip**
>
> It is important to use binding cut on the bias as it needs to ease around the curved corners. If you don't want to make your own, you can buy ready-made bias binding from your local fabric shop.

POT HOLDER

Size: 10½ × 12½in (26.5 × 31.7cm)

PREPARATION:

Strips of fabric are stitched on the diagonal directly on to the wadding (batting) and backing fabric. The pot holder is edged with red bias binding.

> ### Tip
>
> Before stitching the binding to the pot holder ensure that the hanging loop is facing in towards the centre.

CUTTING

All cutting instructions include a ¼in (0.65cm) seam allowance.

Red fabric

- One 10½ × 12½in (26.5 × 31.7cm) rectangle

- Two 1½in (4cm) × width of fabric strips

- One 1½ × 8in (4 × 20.3cm) strip

- 1in × 50in (2.5 × 127cm) bias strip (join to get the required length)

Green fabric

- Two 1½in (4cm) × width of fabric strips

Cream fabric

- Two 1½in (4cm) × width of fabric strips

METHOD

To stitch the pot holder:

1 Lay the wadding (batting) on top of the wrong side of the 10½ x 12½in (26.5 x 31.7cm) red rectangle. The insulated side of the wadding (batting) should be facing the fabric. Pin around the edge to hold in place.

2 Take the strips from all three fabrics. These can be used randomly or in a set order. Lay the first strip on the diagonal from corner to corner, right side up on top of the wadding (batting). Pin in place and trim the strip so that it extends over the outer edge by about 1in (2.5cm) at each end.

3 Place the next strip on top of the first strip right side facing down and stitch along the edge. Flip the fabric strip open so that its right side is now facing upwards. Trim the strip so that it extends over the outer edge by about 1in (2.5cm). Press the strip using your finger or a seam roller. Repeat, working from the centre outwards in each direction until the wadding (batting) is covered. Once you have finished, give it a good press.

4 Turn the unit over so the wrong side is facing up and trim the ends of the strips level with the outer edge of the wadding (batting) and red backing rectangle.

5 To curve the corners, take a large cup or circle template and use it to draw a curved edge on each corner. Cut along the curve.

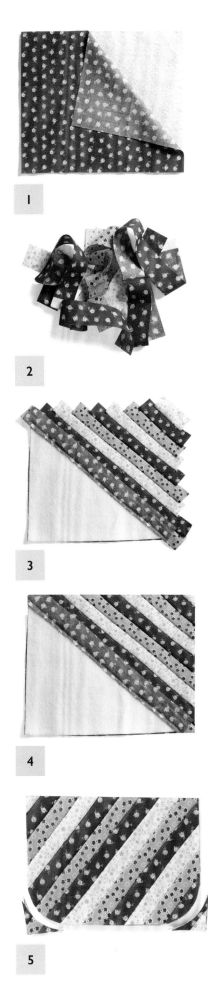

1

2

3

4

5

To stitch the pot holder together:

6 To make the hanging loop, take the 1½ × 8in (4cm × 20.3cm) red strip and fold, then press, under ¼in (0.65cm) along each long side. Fold the strip of fabric wrong sides together so that the folded edges meet. Stitch ⅛in (0.32cm) away from the folded edge. Fold in half and place the two raw ends on one corner of the pot holder. Stitch in place with an ⅛in (0.32cm) seam.

6

7 To make the bias binding, take the 1in × 50in (2.5 × 127cm) red bias strip and fold then iron under ¼in (0.65cm) on one long edge. Turn under one short end and place the raw edge of the binding right side facing the pot holder, matching the raw edges. Stitch around the outer edge of the pot holder. When you get to the place where you started, overlap the binding by ¼in (0.65cm) to hide the raw edge.

7

To finish the pot holder:

8 Fold the binding over the outer edge of the pot holder to the back and slip stitch in place.

8

COFFEE COSY

There is nothing nicer than a colourful cosy to brighten up a breakfast or dinner table. This insulated cover helps to keep the cafetière warm giving you plenty of opportunity for that second cup of piping hot coffee.

SKILL LEVEL: EASY

YOU'LL NEED:

FABRIC

Requirements based on fabrics with a useable width of 107cm (42in):

- 3in (7.5cm) grey fabric for the outer cosy

- 5in (12.7cm) orange print fabric for the lining

- Nine 2 x 1½in (5 x 4cm) rectangles of orange fabric for the patchwork

WADDING (BATTING)

- 14 x 4¾in (35.8 x 12cm) rectangle fusible wadding (batting)

HABERDASHERY

- Grey thread for piecing

- 3½in (8.9cm) strip sew-on hook and loop tape, 1in (2.5cm) wide

Tip

The measurements for this coffee cosy fit a six-cup cafetière, with the edges overlapping by 1½in (4cm) which gives the cover a snug fit. Before starting the project, measure your cafetière to ensure that the cover will fit. If it doesn't then adjust the measurements accordingly.

COFFEE COSY

Size: 13½ × 4¼in (34.3 × 10.8cm)

PREPARATION:

The coffee cosy has a patchwork strip running through the centre and is lined with wadding (batting) and a backing fabric.

> ## Tip
>
> I used fusible wadding (batting) for my cosy but for additional warmth you could use an insulated version instead.

CUTTING

All cutting instructions include a ¼in (0.65cm) seam allowance.

Grey fabric

- One 14 × 2in (35.8 × 5cm) rectangle
- One 14 × 2¼in (35.8 × 5.7cm) rectangle

Orange print fabric

- One 14 × 4¾in (35.8 × 12cm) rectangle

Orange fabrics

From each of the nine orange fabrics cut:

- One 2 × 1½in (5 × 4cm) rectangle

METHOD

To stitch the outer coffee cosy:

1 Lay out the nine 2 × 1½in (5 × 4cm) orange rectangles in a pleasing order and stitch end to end. Press seams one way. Stitch the 14 × 2in (35.8 × 5cm) grey rectangle to the top of the unit and the 14 × 2¼in (35.8 × 5.7cm) grey rectangle to the bottom. Press seams away from the centre.

To stitch the coffee cosy together:

2 Take the loop half of the hook and loop tape and stitch it to the right side of the 14 × 4¾in (35.8 × 12cm) orange print rectangle, ½in (1.3cm) in from the edge of one short end.

3 Iron the fusible wadding (batting) to the wrong side of the orange print rectangle.

4 With right sides together, place the unit completed in Step 2 on top of the unit completed in Step 3 and stitch around each side, leaving a 2in (5cm) gap in stitching on one long edge. Trim corners.

5 Turn the cosy through the gap so it is right side out. Press carefully and topstitch around each side ⅛in (0.32cm) in from the edge, closing the opening as you go.

To finish the coffee cosy:

6 Stitch the second half of the hook and loop tape to the short edge of the outer cosy, on the opposite end to the other strip of tape.

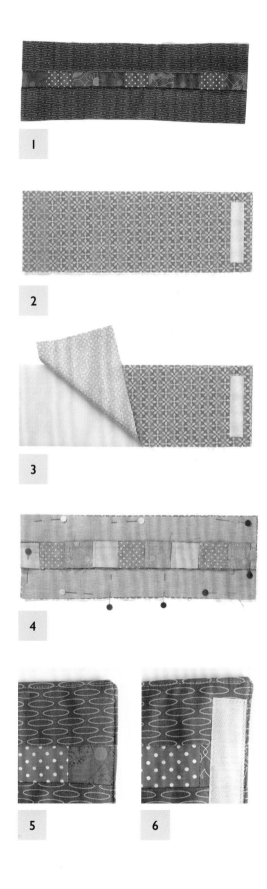

TINY TRAYS

These ever so cute little trays are a speedy make, easily completed in an hour. They are ideal for gifting when filled with something sweet, or perfect for use in the sewing room to keep your thread, buttons and other sewing supplies tidy. The instructions below make one but they are addictive to sew so you may want to cut and sew a batch at a time.

SKILL LEVEL: EASY

YOU'LL NEED:

FABRIC

Requirements based on fabrics with a useable width of 107cm (42in):

- 6½in (16.5cm) square of grey fabric for the outer tray

- Four 3½in (8.9cm) squares of red fabrics for the patchwork

HABERDASHERY

- 6 x 10in (15.2 x 25.4cm) fusible medium weight interfacing

- Grey thread for piecing

- Marking pencil

> **Tip**
>
> It is important that the interfacing is centred accurately on the grey square as this is what gives the tray its structure.

TINY TRAYS

Size: 4in (10.2cm) square

PREPARATION

The tray has a patchwork inner, single fabric outer and interfacing inside to help keep its shape.

Tip

To add a decorative effect, the trays could be embellished with little buttons on the corners.

CUTTING

All cutting instructions include a ¼in (0.65cm) seam allowance.

Grey fabric

- One 6½in (16.5cm) square

Red fabrics

From each of the four red fabrics cut:

- One 3½in (8.9cm) square

Fusible interfacing

- One 5½in (14cm) square
- One 4½in (11.5cm) square

METHOD

To stitch the patchwork:

1 Take the four 3½in (8.9cm) red squares and stitch together into two pairs. Press seams in opposite directions. Sew the pairs together and press seam downwards.

To stitch the tray together:

2 Iron the 5½in (14cm) square of interfacing in the centre of the wrong side of the 6½in (16.5cm) grey square. On top of this, iron the 4½in (11.5cm) square of interfacing, ensuring that it is placed in the centre.

3 Place the unit completed in Step 1 on top of the unit completed in Step 2 with right sides together. Stitch around each side, leaving a 2in (5cm) gap in stitching in the middle of one side. Trim corners and turn the tray through the gap so it is right side out Press carefully then topstitch around each side, ⅛in (0.32cm) in from the edge closing the opening in the side as you go.

To finish the tray:

4 With the patchwork facing upwards, take each corner and fold the fabric in so that each side of the tray is on top of the adjacent side. Measure in 1in (2.5cm) from the corner and draw a line.

5 Stitch on the marked line, from the top to the bottom of the 1in (2.5cm) marking. Reverse the sewing at the start to ensure it is secure.

6 Repeat Steps 4 and 5 to sew the remaining three corners.

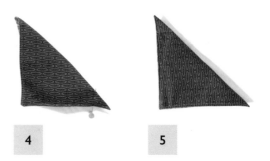

1

2

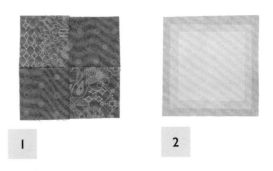

3

4

5

6

DRAUGHT EXCLUDER

Flying geese units stitched in bright fabrics make this draught excluder a colourful, as well as practical, addition to the home. You may wish to choose fabrics to coordinate with your interior, or use leftover fabrics from furnishing projects.

SKILL LEVEL: EASY

YOU'LL NEED:

FABRIC

Requirements based on fabrics with a useable width of 107cm (42in):

- 50cm (20in) light grey for the flying geese and border strips

- One 20.3cm (8in) square each of pink, green, white print and turquoise printed fabrics

HABERDASHERY

- Marking pen or pencil

- Thread for piecing

- Polyester toy filling

Tips

If you have small scraps of wadding (batting) leftover from quilt projects cut them up and use them for stuffing. They provide a really firm filling and so are ideal for this project.

My flying geese all face the same direction but, if you prefer, arrange them in a different format.

DRAUGHT EXCLUDER

Size: 28 × 6in (71 × 15.2cm)

PREPARATION:

The draught excluder is double-sided, with each side made from a strip of eight flying geese. Border strips are then sewn to each edge.

METHOD

To stitch the flying geese units:

1 On the wrong side of the sixteen 3⅞in (9.8cm) light grey squares draw a diagonal line from corner to corner. Take one 7¼in (18.4cm) printed square and two of the 3⅞in (9.8cm) light grey squares. Place the light grey squares on top of the printed square, right sides together, on diagonally opposite corners. Pin, then stitch a scant ¼in (0.65cm) away from each side of the drawn line.

2 Cut along the drawn line to make two units.

CUTTING

All cutting instructions include a ¼in (0.65cm) seam allowance.

Light grey fabric

- Sixteen 3⅞in (9.8cm) squares

- Four 2½ × 6½in (6.3 × 16.5cm) strips

- Four 28½ × 1½in (72.4 × 4cm) strips

Printed fabrics

- One 7¼in (18.4cm) square from each of the four fabrics

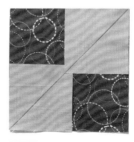

1

2

3 Press seams towards the small triangles. Position another two 3⅞in (9.8cm) light grey squares on the remaining unsewn corner of each unit so that the diagonal line is positioned between the two smaller triangles. Stitch a scant ¼in (0.65cm) away from each side of the drawn line.

4 Cut along the drawn line.

5 Press seams towards the small triangles and trim points. Repeat Steps 1 to 5 with each of the 7¼in (18.4cm) printed squares to make a total of sixteen flying geese units.

To stitch the draught excluder together:

6 Lay out the flying geese units in two rows of eight. Stitch together and press seams in one direction.

7 Stitch a 2½ x 6½in (6.3 x 16.5cm) light grey strip to each end of the two rows of flying geese. Press seams towards the strips. Stitch a 28½ x 1½in (72.4 x 4cm) light grey strip to the top and bottom of each row. Press seams towards the strips.

8 With right sides together, place the two rows on top of each other. Align and pin each edge, then sew along the two long sides and one short side. Trim the corners. Turn the draught excluder right side out and stuff with the polyester toy filling. Close the open end with small, neat slip stitches.

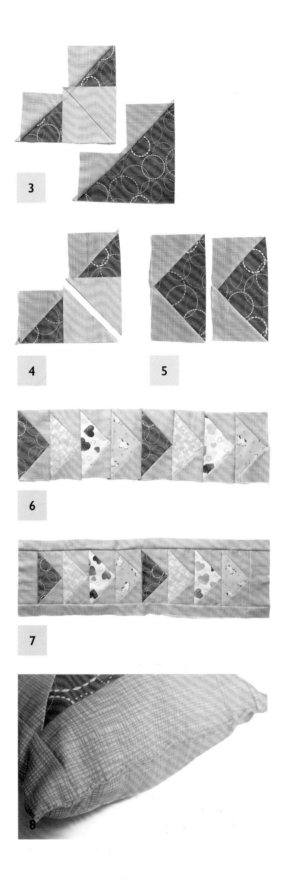

DUVET COVER

Who wouldn't want to sleep under the stars with this crisp, fresh duvet cover. Personalize it by using fabrics that fit in with your bedroom décor or, for a child, you could choose a themed print. I used fabric with a width of 60in (152cm) which avoids having extra seams down the centre of the duvet cover.

SKILL LEVEL: REQUIRES EXPERIENCE

YOU'LL NEED:

FABRIC

Requirements based on fabrics with a useable width of 60in (152cm):

- 105in (266.7cm) white fabric for the patchwork, borders and back

- 66in (167.6cm) turquoise fabric for the front

- 8in (20.3cm) blue print for the patchwork

- 5in (12.7cm) grey print for the patchwork

HABERDASHERY

- Neutral thread for piecing

- 18in (45.7cm) strip of hook and loop sew-on tape, 1in (2.5cm) wide

Tip

As the duvet cover will be subject to lots of use and repeated washing, it is a good idea to neaten and strengthen the seams by sewing a zigzag stitch along the edge of each internal seam line.

DUVET COVER

Size: 54in x 80in (137 x 203cm)

PREPARATION:

The duvet cover is made up of four blocks that each measure 12½in (31.5cm) square, unfinished. The blocks are surrounded by white border strips and framed with a feature fabric.

CUTTING

All cutting instructions include a ¼in (0.65cm) seam allowance.

White fabric

- One 54½ x 81½in (138.4 x 207cm) rectangle

- Two 3½ x 54½in (8.9 x 138.4cm) strips

- Two 3½ x 12½in (8.9 x 31.7cm) strips

- Four 7¼in (18.4cm) squares and cross cut each on the diagonal twice to yield sixteen large triangles

- Eight 3⅞in (9.8cm) squares and cross cut each on the diagonal once to yield sixteen small triangles

- Sixteen 3½in (8.9cm) squares

Turquoise fabric

- One 12½ x 54½in (31.7 x 138.4cm) strip

- One 51½ x 54½in (131 x 138.4cm) rectangle

Blue fabric

- Sixteen 3⅞in (9.8cm) squares and cross cut each on the diagonal once to yield thirty-two small triangles

Grey fabric

- Four 4¾in (12.07cm) squares

METHOD

To stitch one star block:

1 To make the flying geese units, take four large white triangles and eight blue triangles and stitch a blue triangle to one side of each white triangle. Press seams towards the blue triangle. Repeat with the remaining four blue triangles to the other side of the white triangles. Press seams towards the blue triangle. Trim points.

2 Take one grey square and four small white triangles and stitch two triangles to opposite sides of the square. Press seams away from the square. Repeat with the two remaining triangles on the other sides. Trim points.

3 Stitch a unit completed in Step 1 to each side of the unit completed in Step 2. Press seams towards the centre.

4 Take four 3½in (8.9cm) white squares and stitch one to each end of the remaining two units completed in Step 1. Press seams towards the squares.

5 Stitch the units completed in Step 4 to the top and bottom of the unit completed in Step 3. Press seams away from the centre. Repeat to make another three blocks.

Tip

If you prefer, buttons and buttonholes could be substituted for the hook and loop tape.

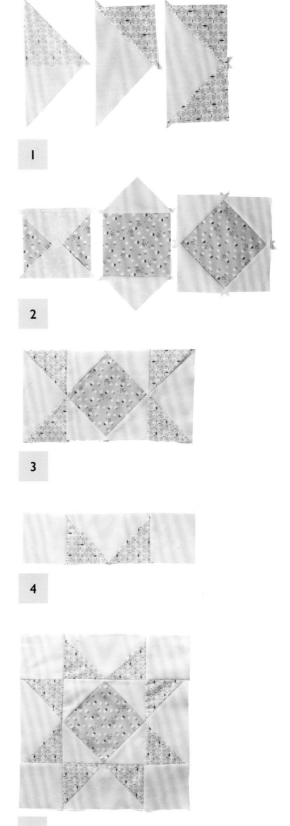

1

2

3

4

5

To stitch the duvet cover together:

6 Lay out the four star blocks in a row and stitch together. Press seams in one direction.

7 Stitch a 3½ × 12½in (8.9 × 31.7cm) white strip to each end of the rows completed in Step 6. Press seams towards the strips. Then stitch a 3½ × 54½in (8.9 × 138.4cm) white strip to the top and bottom of the rows. Press seams towards the strips.

8 Stitch the 12½ × 54½in (31.7 × 138.4cm) turquoise strip to the top of the rows completed in Step 7. Press seam towards the strip. Then stitch the 51½ × 54½in (131 × 138.4cm) turquoise rectangle to the bottom of the rows. Press seam towards the rectangle.

9 With right sides facing, place the duvet top on the 54½ × 81½in (138.4 × 207cm) white rectangle. Pin three sides together, leaving the bottom of the duvet open. Stitch around all three sides. On the bottom edge, fold and press under ¼in (0.65cm) all the way around then fold over 1in (2.5cm) towards the wrong side of the fabric and pin in place. Stitch this down with an ⅛in (0.32cm) seam. Turn the duvet through to the right side and press well.

To finish the duvet cover:

10 Line up the bottom edges, then pin. Cut the hook and loop tape into four equal pieces and position them along the bottom of the duvet, making sure they are evenly spaced. Pull the tape apart and stitch one side of each piece to the inside of the duvet top, aligning the tape with the edge of the duvet as well as the piece of tape opposite. When sewing the tape down, stitch around all four sides so it is secure.

6

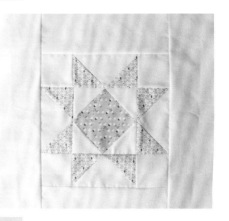

7

8

9   **10**

PILLOWCASE

Match this patchwork star pillowcase with the duvet cover for a crisp look, or stitch as a single project to freshen up a bedroom. Alternatively, a pile of pillows would create a stunning focal point to accompany plain bed linen.

SKILL LEVEL: REQUIRES EXPERIENCE

YOU'LL NEED:

FABRIC

Requirements based on fabrics with a useable width of 107cm (42in):

- 40in (1m) white fabric for the borders, pillowcase back, inner flap and patchwork

- 5in (12.7cm) turquoise fabric for the outer strips

- 4in (10cm) blue print for the patchwork

- 4¾in (12.07cm) square grey print fabric for the patchwork

HABERDASHERY

- Neutral thread for piecing

Tips

As the pillowcase will be subject to lots of use and repeated washing, it is a good idea to neaten and strengthen the seams by sewing a zigzag stitch along the edge of each internal seam line.

If you want to simplify the look of the pillowcase you could use just one patterned fabric with the white.

PILLOWCASE

Size: 20 × 28in (50 × 71cm)

PREPARATION:

The pillowcase features one patchwork star which is surrounded by white borders and turquoise strips. It is finished with a handy envelope opening.

CUTTING

All cutting instructions include a ¼in (0.65cm) seam allowance.

White fabric

- One 20½ × 29½in (52 × 75cm) rectangle
- One 8 × 20½in (20.3 × 52cm) rectangle
- Two 4½ × 12½in (11.5 × 31.7cm) strips
- Two 4½ × 20½in (11.5 × 52cm) strips
- One 7¼in (18.4cm) square and cross cut on the diagonal twice to yield four large triangles
- Two 3⅞in (9.8cm) squares and cross cut each on the diagonal once to yield four small triangles
- Four 3½in (8.9cm) squares

Turquoise fabric

- Two 4½ × 20½in (11.5 × 52cm) strips

Blue print fabric

- Four 3⅞in (9.8cm) squares and cross cut each on the diagonal once to yield eight small triangles

Grey print fabric

- One 4¾in (12.07cm) square

METHOD

To stitch the patchwork:

1 Follow Steps 1 to 5 for the duvet cover to sew one star block.

To stitch the pillowcase together:

2 Sew a 4½ × 12½in (11.5 × 31.7cm) white strip to the top and bottom of the patchwork star. Press seams towards the strips. Then stitch a 4½ × 20½in (11.5 × 52cm) white strip to each side of the unit. Press seams towards the strips.

3 Stitch a 4½ × 20½in (11.5 × 52cm) turquoise strip to each side of the unit completed in Step 2. Press seams towards the strips.

4 To make the inner flap, take the 8 × 20½in (20.3 × 52cm) white rectangle and fold and press under ¼in (0.65cm) on one long side. Stitch the fold down. Sew the opposite long side of the flap to one end of the unit completed in Step 3. Press seam towards the flap.

5 To stitch the back of the pillowcase, take the 20½ × 29½in (52 × 75cm) white rectangle and fold and press under ¼in (0.65cm) on one short side, then fold over another 1in (2.5cm) towards the wrong side of the fabric and pin in place. Stitch with an ⅛in (0.32cm) seam. Place the front and back of the pillowcase right sides together. Line up the stitched edge of the back of the pillowcase with the seam line where the flap joins the pillowcase top. The flap will extend to one side. Pin around three sides of the pillowcase. Fold the flap piece on top of the pillowcase so that you are covering up the opening. Carefully re-pin so that the flap is pinned to all layers of fabric. Stitch around all three sides.

To finish the pillowcase:

6 Turn the pillowcase through so it is right side out and press.

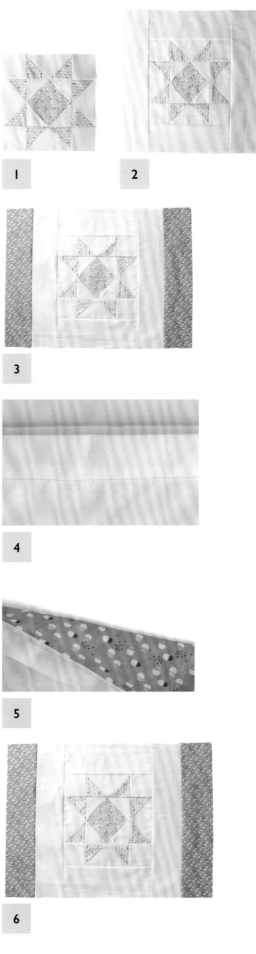

HOT WATER BOTTLE COVER

In the midst of winter there is nothing more comforting than a cosy hot water bottle. This version is quilted which makes it especially warming for snuggling up to on a dark evening. No templates are needed for this project, so the cover will fit most sizes of hot water bottle.

SKILL LEVEL: EASY

YOU'LL NEED:

FABRIC

Requirements based on fabrics with a useable width of 107cm (42in):

- 6in (15.2cm) blue fabric for the outer cover

- 6in (15.2cm) yellow fabric for the patchwork

- 6in (15.2cm) white print fabric for the patchwork

- 12in (30cm) aqua fabric for the lining

WADDING (BATTING)

- 12in (30cm) fusible wadding (batting)

HABERDASHERY

- Neutral thread for piecing
- Grey thread for quilting
- 40in (1m) aqua ribbon, 1in (25mm) wide

Tips

This cover fits a hot water bottle measuring 8 x 13in (20.3 x 33cm). However, there is room within the cover for a slightly larger or smaller hot water bottle.

After sewing the ribbon to the outer section, fold it up and pin it to the patchwork before stitching the outer units together. This will ensure that the ribbon does not get caught in the stitching.

HOT WATER BOTTLE COVER

Size: 10 x 15in (25 x 38cm)

PREPARATION:

The patchwork rectangles extend to both the back and front of the cover, while the lining fabric creates a border around the opening.

CUTTING

All cutting instructions include a ¼in (0.65cm) seam allowance.

Blue fabric

• Four 10½ x 5½in (26.5 x 14cm) rectangles

Yellow fabric

• Five 2½ x 5½in (6.3 x 14cm) rectangles

White print fabric

• Five 2½ x 5½in (6.3 x 14cm) rectangles

Aqua fabric

• Two 10½ x 15½in (26.5 x 39.4cm) rectangles

Fusible wadding (batting)

• Two 10½ x 15½in (26.5 x 39.4cm) rectangles

METHOD

To stitch the patchwork:

1 Stitch the 2½ × 5½in (6.3 × 14cm) yellow and white print rectangles together into two sets of five rectangles. Press seams one way.

2 Stitch a 10½ × 5½in (26.5 × 14cm) blue rectangle to the top and bottom of the units completed in Step 1. Press seams towards the blue rectangles.

To stitch the hot water bottle cover together:

3 Iron the fusible wadding (batting) to the wrong side of each of the units completed in Step 2. Quilt vertical lines from top to bottom through both the fabric and the wadding (batting). Use the pieced strip across the centre as a guide, and quilt both sides of each seam, about ½in (1.3cm) away from the line. Fold the ribbon in half and place it on the right side of one unit, in the centre, 1in (2.5cm) up from the top of the patchwork.

4 Place the two quilted units right sides together and stitch up each long side and across one short side. Trim corners. Repeat with the two 10½ × 15½in (26.5 × 39.4cm) aqua rectangles to make the lining, but leave a 4in (10cm) gap in stitching in the middle of one side.

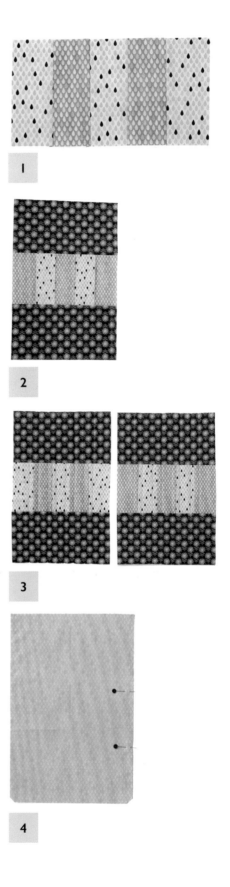

To finish the hot water bottle cover:

5 Turn through the outer hot water bottle cover so that the right side is facing out. Place it inside the lining, right sides together, and pin all the way around the top edge. Sew around this edge, matching the side seams. Turn the hot water bottle cover right side out through the opening in the lining. Stitch the opening closed. Carefully press the top of the hot water bottle cover so that ¼in (0.65cm) of the lining is showing on the outside and pin in place. Stitch through all layers in the seam line around the top.

6 Place your hot water bottle inside the cover and tie the ribbon with a neat bow.

NOTEBOOK COVER

Turn a dull notebook into a treasured possession with this smart and eye-catching cover. The beauty of making your own cover is that, once it is full of shopping lists, recipes or even sewing notes, you can simply take it off and re-use it on your next notebook.

SKILL LEVEL: EASY

YOU'LL NEED:

FABRIC

Requirements based on fabrics with a useable width of 107cm (42in):

- 12in (30cm) green fabric for the notebook outer and the inner flaps

- 10in (25cm) aqua fabric for the lining

- Seven 2¾ x 1¾in (7 x 4.4cm) blue strips

HABERDASHERY

- Neutral thread for piecing

- 10in (25cm) medium weight fusible interfacing

- 6 x 8½in (15.2 x 21.6cm) notebook

Tip

The instructions can be adjusted to make a cover to fit a different sized notebook. To do this, measure the width of the book including the front, moving around the spine and then to the back. Add 1in (2.5cm) to this measurement. Measure the height of the notebook and add 1in (2.5cm) to this measurement. This gives you the cutting measurements for the front cover, lining and interfacing. To calculate the measurement for the flaps use the same height measurement as the front cover and keep the width the same as the pattern.

NOTEBOOK COVER

Size: 6¼ × 8¾in (15.8 × 22.2cm)

PREPARATION:

The notebook cover has a strip of patchwork across the centre, a contrast lining and a flap at each side to tuck around the notebook.

CUTTING

All cutting instructions include a ¼in (0.65cm) seam allowance.

Green fabric

- Two 4½ × 13½in (11.5 × 34.3cm) rectangles

- Two 7½ × 9½in (19 × 24cm) rectangles

Aqua fabric

- One 13½ × 9½in (34.3 × 24cm) rectangle

- One 2in (5cm) square

Blue fabric scraps

- Seven 2½ × 1½in (6.3 × 4cm) blue strips

Fusible interfacing

- One 13½ × 9½in (34.3 × 24cm) rectangle

METHOD

To stitch the patchwork:

1 Stitch the seven 2½ × 1½in (6.3 × 4cm) blue strips together end to end, then trim an equal amount from each end so the strip measures 13½ × 1½in (34.3 × 4cm). Press seams one way.

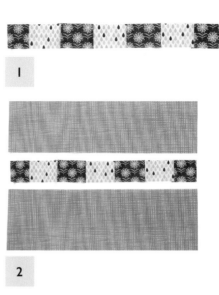

2 Stitch a 3½ × 4½in (34.3 × 11.5cm) green rectangle to the top and bottom of the unit completed in Step 1. Press seams towards the green rectangles. Iron the fusible interfacing to the reverse of this unit.

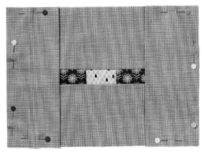

To stitch the notebook cover together:

3 To make the inner flaps fold each of the 7½ × 9½in (19 × 24cm) green rectangles in half vertically, wrong sides together, and press. Place an inner flap on each end of the right side of the notebook cover so that the raw edges line up and the folded edge faces the centre.

4 Lay the 13½ × 9½in (34.3 × 24cm) aqua rectangle on top of the cover, right sides together. Pin around the outer edge then stitch around all four sides, leaving a 3in (7.5cm) gap in stitching on one long side.

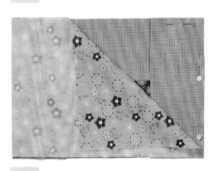

To finish the notebook cover:

5 Trim the corners and turn the cover through the gap so it is right side out. Push out the corners and give it a press. Close the opening with small, neat slip stitches and place on your notebook.

LAP QUILT

Sometimes you have a selection of fabrics that just need to be shown off with a simple design. This project does just that and, with clever piecing, this quilt grows very quickly. It is an ideal size for throwing over the sofa, keeping in the car or taking out on a picnic.

SKILL LEVEL: EASY

YOU'LL NEED:

FABRIC

Requirements based on fabrics with a useable width of 107cm (42in):

- 60in (1½m) white fabric for the patchwork and backing

- 22in (56cm) light grey fabric for the patchwork and outer borders

- 20in (50cm) dark grey fabric for the patchwork and binding

- 5in (12.7cm) lime green fabric for the patchwork

- 5in (12.7cm) green fabric for the patchwork

- 10in (25.4cm) mustard fabric for the patchwork and inner borders

WADDING (BATTING)

- 38 x 44in (96.5 x 112cm) wadding (batting)

HABERDASHERY

- Neutral thread for piecing
- Grey thread for quilting

LAP QUILT

Size: 35½ × 41½in (90 × 105.4cm)

PREPARATION:

The quilt centre is made up of seven columns, with each one containing seventeen rectangles. The placement of the fabrics creates the staggered effect.

CUTTING

All cutting instructions include a ¼in (0.65cm) seam allowance.

White fabric

- One 38 × 44in (96.5 × 112cm) rectangle

- Thirty 4½ × 2½in (11.5 × 6.3cm) rectangles

Light grey fabric

- Two 3 × 36½in (7.5 × 92.7cm) strips

- Two 3 × 35½in (7.5 × 90cm) strips

- Thirty 4½ × 2½in (11.5 × 6.3cm) rectangles

Dark grey fabric

- Four 2in (5cm) × width of fabric strips

- Thirty 4½ × 2½in (11.5 × 6.3cm) rectangles

Lime green fabric

- Eleven 4½ × 2½in (11.5 × 6.3cm) rectangles

Green fabric

- Eleven 4½ × 2½in (11.5 × 6.3cm) rectangles

Mustard fabric

- Two 1½ × 34½in (4 × 87.6cm) strips

- Two 1½ × 30½in (4 × 77.4cm) strips

- Seven 4½ × 2½in (11.5 × 6.3cm) rectangles

METHOD

To stitch the patchwork:

1 Take all the 4½ × 2½in (11.5 × 6.3cm) fabric rectangles and lay them out into a grid of seven across and seventeen down. Refer to the photos for placement. In each row the fabrics move up one step to create the staggered effect. Pin and stitch the rectangles into seven columns.

2 Press seams in each column in opposite directions.

3 Stitch the columns together, pinning to match the seams. Press seams in one direction.

To add the borders:

4 The quilt has two borders. After stitching each strip press the seam towards the strip. To add the inner border, sew a 1½ × 34½in (4 × 87.6cm) mustard strip to opposite sides of the quilt top followed by a 1½ × 30½in (4 × 77.4cm) mustard strip to the top and bottom. To add the outer border, sew a 3 × 36½in (7.5 × 92.7cm) light grey strip to opposite sides of the quilt top followed by a 3 × 35½in (7.5 × 90cm) light grey strip to the top and bottom.

> *Tip*
>
> Once you have pinned the rectangles together into columns, label each one with a number. This will help to avoid any confusion when you stitch them together.

1

2

3

4

To finish the quilt:

5 Layer the quilt by placing the 38 x 44in (96.5 x 112cm) rectangle of white backing fabric wrong side up on a flat surface, followed by the wadding (batting) and then the quilt top, centrally placed and right side up. Secure the quilt sandwich with tacking (basting) stitches or quilters' pins placed at regular intervals. The wadding (batting) and backing will be slightly larger than the patchwork top. The quilt is machine quilted with grey thread in vertical and horizontal lines in the ditch (in each seam line) across the quilt. The quilting continues from the seam lines to the outer border. When you have finished quilting trim the excess backing and wadding (batting) level with quilt top edges.

6 To add the binding, stitch the dark grey binding strips together to form one continuous strip. Press seams open to reduce bulk. Fold the strip in half lengthwise, wrong sides together, and press. Match the raw edges of the binding to the raw edges of the quilt and sew in place. Fold the binding over to the back of the quilt and neatly slip stitch in place.

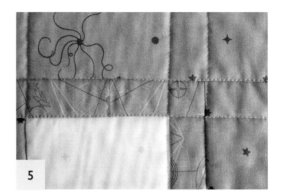

5

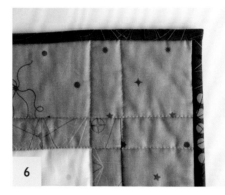

6

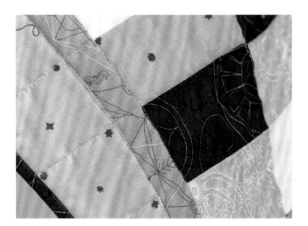

Tip

If you are not a confident quilter then quilting by stitching in the ditch is a great technique as the quilting sinks into the seam lines.

CROSS CUSHION

Mustard, grey and white fabric combinations are so on trend at the moment which makes this cushion a perfect accessory in a modern living room. Make it in fabrics that complement your décor or choose contrasting colours to create a statement piece.

SKILL LEVEL: REQUIRES EXPERIENCE

YOU'LL NEED:

FABRIC

Requirements based on fabrics with a useable width of 107cm (42in):

- 8in (20.3cm) white fabric for the patchwork and inner border

- 8in (20.3cm) mustard fabric for the patchwork

- 30in (76cm) grey fabric for the patchwork, outer border and cushion back

- 18½in (47cm) cream fabric for the inner backing

WADDING (BATTING)

- 18½in (47cm) square wadding (batting)

HABERDASHERY

- Neutral thread for piecing
- Pale grey thread for quilting
- 18in (45.7cm) square cushion pad

CROSS CUSHION

Size: 18in (45.7cm) square

PREPARATION:

The centre block is surrounded by an inner and outer border. The cover is quilted with vertical straight-line quilting and finished with an easy envelope back.

CUTTING

All cutting instructions include a ¼in (0.65cm) seam allowance.

White fabric

- One 2⅝ × 6⅞in (6.7 × 17.5cm) rectangle
- Two 2⅝in (6.7cm) squares
- Two 1½ × 12½in (4 × 31.75cm) strips
- Two 1½ × 14½in (4 × 37cm) strips

Mustard fabric

- Four 2⅝ × 6⅞in (6.7 ×17.5cm) rectangles
- Eight 2⅝in (6.7cm) squares

Grey fabric

- Two 18½ × 13¼in (47 × 33.6cm) rectangles
- Three 4¼in (10.8cm) squares and cross cut each on the diagonal twice to yield twelve large triangles
- Two 2⅝in (6.7cm) squares and cross cut each on the diagonal once to yield four small triangles
- Two 2½ × 14½in (6.3 × 37cm) strips
- Two 2½ × 18½in (6.3 × 47cm) strips

Cream fabric

- One 18½in (47cm) square

METHOD

To stitch the patchwork:

1 Take two 2⅝in (6.7cm) mustard squares and stitch them to each side of a 2⅝in (6.7cm) white square. Press seams towards the mustard square. Repeat with another three squares.

2 Stitch the units made in Step 1 to each side of a 2⅝ × 6⅞in (6.7 × 17.5cm) white rectangle. Press seams towards the rectangle.

3 Stitch a 2⅝ × 6⅞in (6.7 × 17.5cm) mustard rectangle to each side of the unit completed in Step 2. Press seams towards the rectangle.

4 Take the remaining four 2⅝in (6.7cm) mustard squares and stitch a large grey triangle to one side. Press seam towards the triangle. Repeat on the opposite side. On the third side of each unit, stitch a small grey triangle. Press seam towards the triangle. Trim points.

Tip

The most economical way to cut the grey fabric is to start with the two rectangles for the back of the cushion then use the remaining fabric for the smaller patchwork pieces.

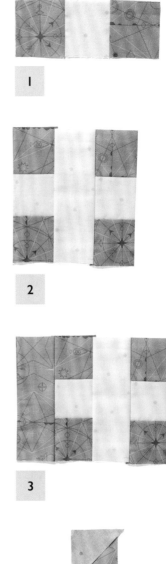

1

2

3

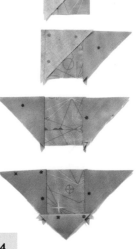

4

5 Take two of the units completed in Step 4 and stitch to each end of the unit completed in Step 3. Press seams towards the rectangle.

6 Take the remaining two $2\frac{5}{8} \times 6\frac{7}{8}$in (6.7 ×17.5cm) mustard rectangles and stitch a large grey triangle to each end. Press seams towards the triangles.

7 Stitch each of the units completed in Step 6 to the remaining two units completed in Step 4. Press seams towards the rectangles. Trim points. Stitch these units to each side of the unit completed in Step 5 matching the seams carefully. Press seams away from the centre.

To stitch the cushion together:

8 Stitch a $1\frac{1}{2} \times 12\frac{1}{2}$in (4 × 31.75cm) white border strip to opposite sides of the cushion top. Press seams towards the border. Then sew a $1\frac{1}{2} \times 14\frac{1}{2}$in (4 × 37cm) white border strip to the top and bottom of the cushion top and press seams towards the border.

9 Stitch a $2\frac{1}{2} \times 14\frac{1}{2}$in (6.3 × 37cm) grey border strip to opposite sides of the cushion top. Press seams towards the border. Then sew a $2\frac{1}{2} \times 18\frac{1}{2}$in (6.3 × 47cm) grey border strip to the top and bottom of the cushion top. Press seams towards the border.

Tip

When quilting the vertical lines across the cushion, mark a centre line first and then stitch the lines from the centre. This helps to keep them straight.

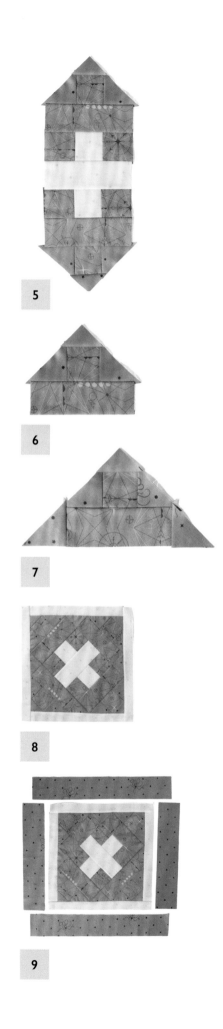

To finish the cushion:

10 Layer the cushion top by placing the 18½in (47cm) square of cream fabric wrong side up on a surface, followed by the wadding (batting) and then the cushion top, centrally and right side up. Secure the quilt sandwich with tacking (basting) stitches or quilters' pins placed at regular intervals. Using pale grey thread, machine quilt vertical lines ½in (1.3cm) apart across the cushion top.

11 To stitch the envelope back for the cushion, take the two 18½ × 13¼in (47 × 33.6cm) grey rectangles and, on one 18½in (47cm) edge of each, fold and press ¼in (0.65cm) towards the wrong side. Fold this edge again, by 2in (5cm) to create a hem, press then sew in place. Position one backing piece on the cushion front right sides together with the folded edge in the middle and pin around the outer edge. Repeat with the second backing piece. Stitch around the outer edge of the cushion. Trim corners, turn through so the right side is facing out and insert the cushion pad.

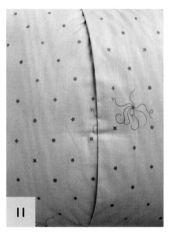

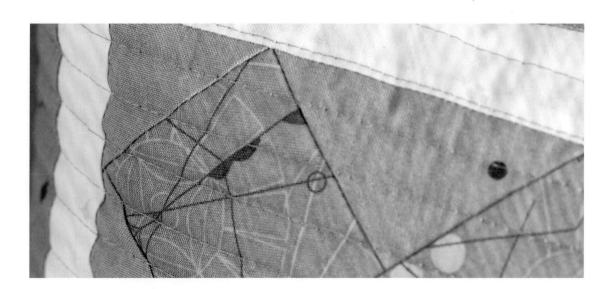

FLOOR CUSHION

This cushion is great for relaxing on while watching TV, reading or just putting on the sofa for snuggling down. The vibrant lime colourway accompanied by the dark grey background means the crosses really do appear to pop out of the cushion.

SKILL LEVEL: REQUIRES EXPERIENCE

YOU'LL NEED:

FABRIC

Requirements based on fabrics with a useable width of 107cm (42in):

- 70in (1¾m) dark grey for the background, borders and back of cushion

- 15in (38cm) lime green and white for the crosses

- 15in (38cm) bright green for the crosses

- 32in (81.3cm) plain cream for the inner backing

WADDING (BATTING)

- 32in (81.3cm) square wadding (batting)

HABERDASHERY

- Neutral thread for piecing

- Dark grey thread for quilting

- 28in (71cm) square cushion pad

Tips

There are lots of seams to match in the patchwork but if you press them as indicated in the instructions they will nest together and match perfectly.

If you are not confident quilting diagonal lines then try quilting in the ditch. This can look very effective and you don't have the worry of getting your lines of quilting straight as you follow the seam line. This creates a quilted effect without seeing the actual quilting.

FLOOR CUSHION

Size: 30in (76cm) square

PREPARATION:

The cushion centre is made up of four blocks. Each block measures 12½in (31.5cm) unfinished. The blocks are stitched together and an outer border added.

CUTTING

All cutting instructions include a ¼in (0.65cm) seam allowance.

Dark grey fabric

- Twenty 2⅝in (6.7cm) squares

- Twelve 4¼in (10.8cm) squares and cross cut each on the diagonal twice to yield forty-eight large triangles

- Eight 2⅜in (6cm) squares and cross cut each on the diagonal one to yield sixteen small triangles

- Two 3½ x 24½in (8.9 x 62.3cm) strips

- Two 3½ x 30½in (8.9 x 77.5cm) strips

- One 30½in (77.5cm) square

Lime green and white fabric

- Eight 2⅝ x 6⅞in (6.7 x 17.5cm) rectangles

- Sixteen 2⅝in (6.7cm) squares

Bright green fabric

- Eight 2⅝ x 6⅞in (6.7 x 17.5cm) rectangles

- Sixteen 2⅝in (6.7cm) squares

METHOD

To make the patchwork:

1 Take two 2⅝ x 6⅞in (6.7 x 17.5cm) lime green and white rectangles and one 2⅝in (6.7cm) dark grey square and stitch the square between the rectangles. Press seams towards the square. Stitch a small dark grey triangle to each end. Press seams towards the triangles.

2 Take two 2⅝ x 6⅞in (6.7 x 17.5cm) bright green rectangles and stitch a small dark grey triangle to one end. Press seams towards the triangle.

3 Take two 2⅝in (6.7cm) dark grey squares and two 2⅝in (6.7cm) lime green and white squares and stitch together in pairs. Press seams towards the dark grey squares. Stitch a large dark grey triangle to one end of each unit.

4 Take two 2⅝in (6.7cm) bright green squares and four large dark grey triangles and stitch a large dark grey triangle to one side of each square. Press seam away from the square. Repeat to sew another large dark grey triangle on the adjacent side.

5 Stitch the units made in Steps 3 and 4 together. Press seams towards the unit with two triangles. This makes two diagonally opposite corners for one block.

6 Take two 2⅝in (6.7cm) dark grey squares and two 2⅝in (6.7cm) lime green and white squares and stitch together in pairs. Press seams towards the dark grey squares. Stitch a large dark grey triangle to one end of each unit. Note that the triangle is stitched in the opposite direction to those stitched in Step 3.

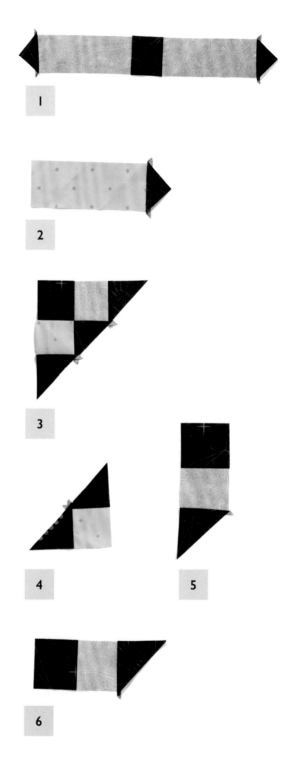

7 Take two 2⅝in (6.7cm) bright green squares and four large dark grey triangles and stitch a large dark grey triangle to one side of each square. Press seam away from the square. Repeat with a second large dark grey triangle on the adjacent side. Stitch these units, and the ones made in Step 6 together. Press seams towards the unit with two triangles. This makes the second two diagonally opposite corners for one block. Stitch a unit completed in Step 2 between the units completed in Step 5 and 7. Press seams away from the centre.

8 Stitch the unit completed in Step 1 between the units completed in Step 7. Press seams away from the centre. Repeat Steps 1 to 8 to make another three blocks.

7

8

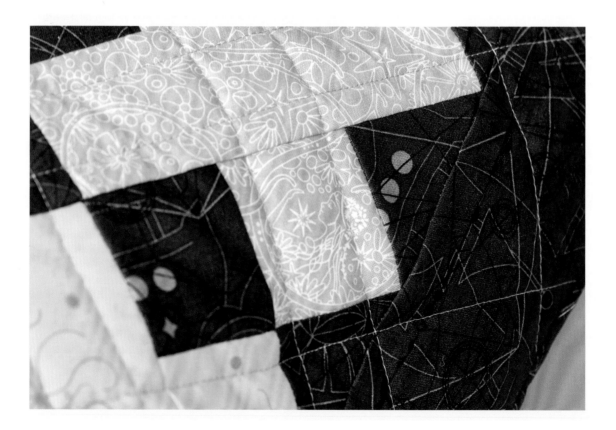

To stitch the cushion together:

9 Lay out the four blocks and stitch together into two rows. Press the seams in each row in opposite directions, then stitch the rows together. Press all seams downwards. Stitch a 3½ × 24½in (8.9 × 62.3cm) dark grey strip to opposite sides of the cushion top. Press seams towards the border. Then stitch a 3½ × 30½in (8.9 × 77.5cm) dark grey strip to the top and bottom of the cushion top. Press seams towards the border.

To finish the cushion:

10 Layer the cushion top by placing the 32in (81.3cm) square of cream fabric wrong side up on a surface, followed by the wadding (batting) and then the cushion top, centrally positioned and right side up. The backing and wadding (batting) are slightly larger than the cushion top. Secure the quilt sandwich with tacking (basting) stitches or quilters' pins placed at regular intervals. Quilt the cushion front. I used a dark grey thread to quilt diagonal lines ½in (1.3cm) in from the outer edge of each cross in both directions.

11 Trim the excess backing and wadding (batting) level with the edge of the cushion front. Place the 30½in (77.5cm) dark grey square on top of the cushion front, right sides together, and pin around each edge. Stitch around all four sides, leaving a 12in (30cm) gap in stitching in the middle of one side. Trim corners and turn through so the right side is facing out. Insert the cushion pad and close the opening with small, neat slip stitches.

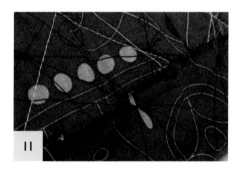

BED QUILT

A bright, fresh, modern quilt for everyday use. This is a weekend project with a difference, one weekend to stitch the patchwork then one weekend to quilt and bind. The repeated nature of the construction means that once you have stitched the first few blocks, the rest will follow very quickly.

SKILL LEVEL: REQUIRES EXPERIENCE

YOU'LL NEED:

FABRIC

Requirements based on fabrics with a useable width of 107cm (42in):

- 120in (3m) white fabric for the background, joining strips and borders

- 8in (20.3cm) each of six graded purple fabrics for the patchwork

- 58 × 60in (147.3 × 152cm) backing fabric

- 12in (30.5cm) binding fabric

WADDING (BATTING)

- 58 × 60in (147.3 × 152cm) wadding (batting)

HABERDASHERY

- Neutral thread for piecing
- White thread for quilting

Tip

When sewing the white joining strips to the rows of blocks, stitch the seam with the blocks facing upwards. This way you can see where the seams intersect and so are less likely to lose any points in the seam line.

BED QUILT

Size: 54½ x 57½in (138.4 x 146cm)

PREPARATION:

The quilt centre is made up of six rows, with each row containing eight blocks. The rows are separated with strips of white fabric which are framed with a white border.

CUTTING

All cutting instructions include a ¼in (0.65cm) seam allowance.

White fabric

* Two 3½ x 57½in (8.9 x 146cm) strips (cut from the length of the fabric)

* Seven 3½ x 48½in (8.9 x 123cm) strips (cut from the length of the fabric)

* Twelve 7¼in (18.4cm) squares

* Forty-eight 3⅞in (9.8cm) squares

Purple fabrics

* From each of the six purple fabrics cut:

* Two 7¼in (18.4cm) squares

* Eight 3⅞in (9.8cm) squares

Binding fabric

* Six 2in (5cm) x width of fabric strips

METHOD

To stitch the patchwork:

1 To stitch one row take the two 7¼in (18.4cm) squares cut from the darkest purple fabric and eight 3⅞in (9.8cm) white squares. Draw a diagonal line from corner to corner on the wrong side of the white squares. Place two of the white squares on top of each purple square, right sides together, on diagonally opposite corners. Pin, then stitch ¼in (0.65cm) away from each side of the drawn line.

2 Cut along the drawn line to make two units.

3 Press seams towards the small triangles.

4 Position another two white squares on the remaining unsewn corner of each unit so that the diagonal line is positioned between the two smaller triangles. Stitch ¼in (0.65cm) away from each side of the drawn line. Cut along the drawn line and press seams towards the small triangles and trim points. These units make the upper part of each block.

5 To make the lower units take the two 7¼in (18.4cm) white squares and eight 3⅞in (9.8cm) squares cut from the darkest purple fabric and repeat Steps 1 to 5. Stitch each upper unit to the top of a lower unit. Press the seams upwards on four blocks and downwards on the remaining four blocks. To make the rest of the blocks, repeat Steps 1 to 5 with the remaining five purple fabrics.

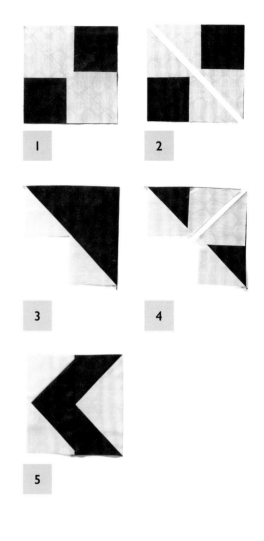

1

2

3

4

5

Tip

The fabrics in this quilt are graded from light to dark but the design would work equally well with each row being made from a different colour fabric.

To stitch the pieced blocks together:

6 Stitch the eight blocks of the darkest purple fabric together in a row, alternating the blocks so that the pressed seams alternate between up and down. Press seams one way. Repeat with the remaining five purple fabrics.

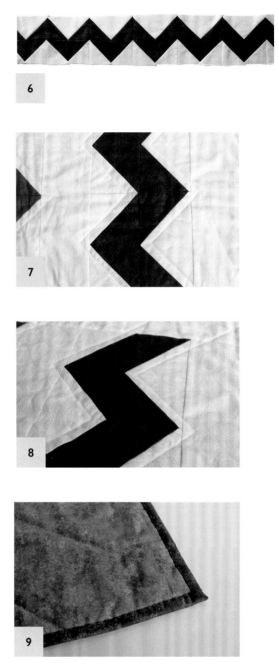

7 Take the seven 3½ × 48½in (8.9 × 123cm) white strips and stitch one between each row of purple blocks and at the top and bottom. Press seams towards the strips. Stitch a 3½ × 57½in (8.9 × 146cm) white strip to opposite sides of the quilt. Press seams towards the border strips.

To finish the quilt:

8 Layer the quit by placing the 58 × 60in (147.3 × 152cm) rectangle of backing fabric wrong side up on a clean surface, followed by the wadding (batting) and then the quilt top, centrally placed and right side up. Secure the quilt sandwich with tacking (basting) stitches or quilters' pins placed at regular intervals. The wadding (batting) and backing will be slightly larger than the patchwork top. The quilt is machine quilted with white thread ½in (1.3cm) away from the purple fabrics that zigzag across the quilt. The quilting is extended out from the seam lines to the outer border. When you have finished quilting trim the excess backing and wadding (batting) level with the edges of the quilt top.

9 Stitch the binding strips together to form one continuous strip. Press seams open to reduce bulk. Fold the strip in half lengthwise, wrong sides together, and press. Match the raw edges of the binding to the raw edges of the quilt and sew in place. Fold the binding over to the back of the quilt and neatly slip stitch in place by hand.

LAUNDRY BAG

This lovely laundry bag is fully lined and roomy enough for even the largest stash of washing. It is particularly handy when travelling as it can fold down to fit in even the smallest space in your case. The drawstring top allows the bag to neatly hang up out of the way.

SKILL LEVEL: EASY

YOU'LL NEED

FABRIC

Requirements based on fabrics with a useable width of 107cm (42in):

- 30in (76.2cm) light blue for the outer bag

- 10in (25cm) navy for the patchwork and drawstrings

- 25in (63.5cm) plain blue for the lining

HABERDASHERY

- Light blue thread

- Large safety pin for threading

- Marking pen or pencil

> *Tip*
>
> Not only does this pattern make a laundry bag, but it could also be used for a sports kit or books.

LAUNDRY BAG

Size: 18 x 24in (45.7 x 61cm)

PREPARATION

Both outer sides of the laundry bag have the same patchwork detail. The lining uses a plain fabric.

CUTTING

All cutting instructions include a 0.65cm (¼in) seam allowance.

Light blue fabric

- Four 3½in (8.9cm) squares

- Four 2 x 3½in (5 x 8.9cm) rectangles

- Six 18½ x 2½in (47 x 6.3cm) strips

- Two 18½ x 14in (47 x 35.8cm) rectangles

Navy fabric

- Six 3½in (8.9cm) squares

- Four 18½ x 1½in (47 x 4cm) strips

- Two 1½ x 40in (4 x 101.6cm) strips

Plain blue fabric

- Two 18½ x 24½in (47 x 62.2cm) rectangles

METHOD

To stitch the outer bag

1 To sew one side of the outer bag, take three 3½in (8.9cm) navy squares and two 3½in (8.9cm) light blue squares and stitch together, alternating the fabrics. Stitch a 2 × 3½in (5 × 8.9cm) light blue rectangle to each end. Press seams towards the navy fabric.

2 Stitch an 18½ × 2½in (47 × 6.3cm) light blue strip to the top and bottom of the unit completed in Step 1. Press seams towards the strip.

3 Stitch an 18½ × 1½in (47 × 4cm) navy strip to the top and bottom of the unit completed in Step 2. Press seams towards the navy strip.

4 Stitch an 18½ × 2½in (47 × 6.3cm) light blue strip to the bottom of the unit completed in Step 3 and an 18½ × 14in (47 × 35.8cm) light blue rectangle to the top. Press seams towards the navy fabrics. Repeat Steps 1 to 4 to make the second side of the outer bag.

5 On both long sides of each outer bag panel, measure and mark 2in (5cm) and 3in (7.5cm) from the top on the outer edge. Place the outer bag panels right sides together and pin each side and across the bottom, matching the seams. Do not pin between the 2in (5cm) and 3in (7.5cm) markings. Stitch down each side, stopping the stitching between the markings and stitching across the bottom of the bag. Press seams open and clip corners.

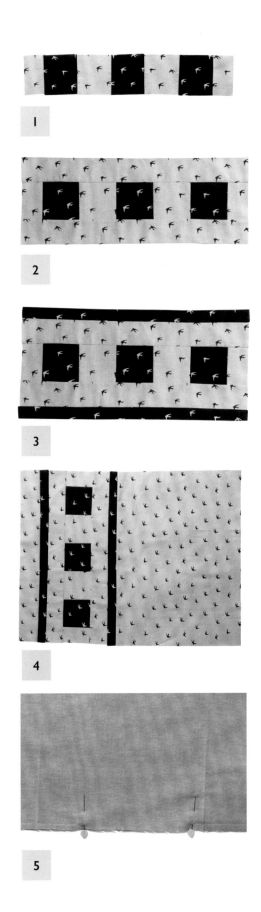

1

2

3

4

5

To stitch the lining

6 Take the two 18½ × 24½in (47 × 62.2cm) plain blue rectangles. Place them right sides together and stitch down each side and across the bottom, leaving a 5in (12.7cm) gap for turning in the bottom. Trim corners.

To stitch the drawstring ties:

7 Take the two 1½ × 40in (4 × 101.6cm) navy strips and fold, then press under ¼in (0.65cm) along each long side. Fold the strip of fabric wrong sides together so that the folded edges meet. Stitch ⅛in (0.32cm) away from the folded edge.

To stitch the bag together:

8 With the right side facing outwards, put the outer bag inside the lining so that the right side of the lining is facing the right side of the bag. Pin around the top, making sure the side seams are aligned, and then stitch all the way around. Turn the bag through the gap in the lining. Push out the corners and stitch the gap closed. Press and topstitch around the top edge, ⅛in (0.32cm) away from the top of the bag.

9 To stitch the casing for the drawstrings, measure 1¾in (4.4cm) down from the top of the bag and draw a line horizontally across the bag on both sides. Draw another line 1in (2.5cm) away from this line. These lines should align with the 1in (2.5cm) gaps left in the bag side seams. Stitch along both of these drawn lines.

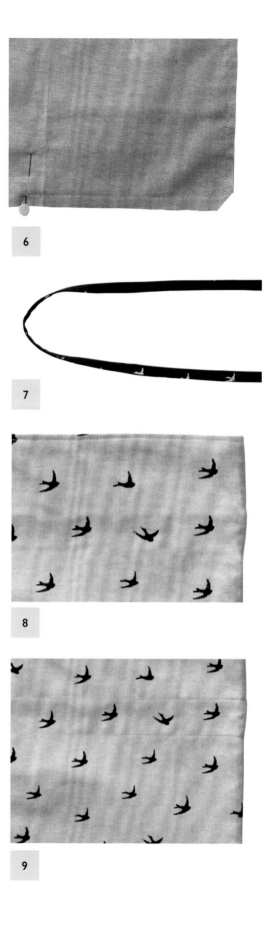

6

7

8

9

10 Attach the safety pin to one end of one of the drawstring ties. Starting on the right-hand side, thread one drawstring through the front casing, back through the back casing and tie the ends in a knot on the right side. Repeat the process with the second drawstring but this time start on the left-hand side.

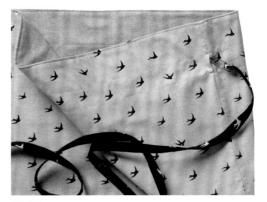

10

Tip

If time is short and you need to speed up the making time, you could just make the patchwork feature for the front of the bag and keep the back plain.

STORAGE BASKETS

These baskets will look pretty on your shelves as well as providing handy storage for sewing supplies, stationery or cosmetics. Much of the lining fabric can be seen so, when choosing fabrics, make sure that you select colours or prints that complement each other.

SKILL LEVEL: REQUIRES EXPERIENCE

SMALL BASKET YOU'LL NEED:

FABRIC

Requirements based on fabrics with a useable width of 107cm (42in):

- 12in (30.5cm) dark blue for the outer base and lining

- 10in (25cm) light blue for the outer basket and handles

WADDING (BATTING)

- 9½ x 12in (24 x 30.5cm) fusible wadding (batting)

HABERDASHERY

- Light blue thread

- Dark blue thread

> **Tip**
>
> When choosing the fabric for the lining and the outer base it is best not to use a directional print. The fabric folds around the basket so it would end up being upside down on the second side.

STORAGE BASKETS

Size:
Small basket 9 × 4½ × 2¼in
(23 × 11.5 × 5.7cm)

Large basket 12½ × 7 × 3¼in
(31.5 × 17.8 × 7.6cm)

PREPARATION

These baskets are made from just a few pieces of fabric so there is not much to prepare. If you assemble all your supplies before starting, it will make your sewing super speedy.

CUTTING (SMALL BASKET)

All cutting instructions include a 0.65cm (¼in) seam allowance.

Dark blue fabric

- One 9½ × 6in (24 × 15.2cm) rectangle
- One 9½ × 11½in (24 × 29cm) rectangle

Light blue fabric

- Two 9½ × 3½in (24 × 8.9cm) rectangles
- One 3½ × 11½in (8.9 × 29cm) strip

METHOD

To stitch the outer basket and handles:

1 Stitch a 9½ × 3½in (24 × 8.9cm) light blue rectangle to each side of the 9½ × 6in (24 × 15.2cm) dark blue rectangle. Press seams away from the centre.

2 Iron the fusible wadding (batting) to the wrong side of the unit completed in Step 1. Using dark blue thread, stitch in the ditch along both seam lines through the fabric and wadding (batting).

3 Fold the basket in half with right sides together. Stitch down each side.

4 To shape the base match the centre base line with the side seam. Measure in 1¼in (3.1cm) along the seam line and stitch across.

5 Cut off the excess fabric. Repeat to cut off the excess fabric at the opposite corner then turn through.

6 To make the handles, take the 3½ × 11½in (8.9 × 29cm) strip of light blue fabric and fold then press under ¼in (0.65cm) along each long side.

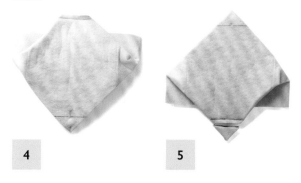

> ### Tip
>
> The handles could be made longer if you wanted to use the basket for carrying rather than for storage.

7 Fold the strip of fabric wrong sides together so that the folded edges meet. Stitch ⅛in (0.32cm) away from the folded edge. Stitch ⅛in (0.32cm) away from the long edge on the other side. Cut in half to make the two handles.

8 Take the basket and turn through so the right side is facing out. With right sides facing, place the raw edges of each handle on either side of the basket side seam. Pin and then stitch the handles to the basket using an ⅛in (0.32cm) seam.

To stitch the lining:

9 To stitch the lining take the 9½ x 11½in (24 x 29cm) dark blue rectangle and fold in half, right sides facing, with the 9½in (24cm) opening at the top. Stitch down each side but leave a 2½in (6.3cm) gap in stitching on one side, approximately 1½in (4cm) from the top.

10 To shape the lining corners, match the centre base line with the side seam. Measure in 1¼in (3.1cm) along the seam line and stitch across. Cut off the excess fabric ¼in (0.65cm) away from the sewn line. Repeat on the other corner.

To stitch the basket together:

11 Turn the outer basket so that the wadding (batting) is facing outwards. Put the lining inside the basket so that the right side of the lining is facing the right side of the basket. Pin around the top matching the side seams and then stitch all the way around.

12 Turn the basket through the gap in stitching in the lining. Push out the corners and stitch the gap closed with the dark blue thread. Press and topstitch around the edge, ⅛in (0.32cm) in from the top using the light blue thread.

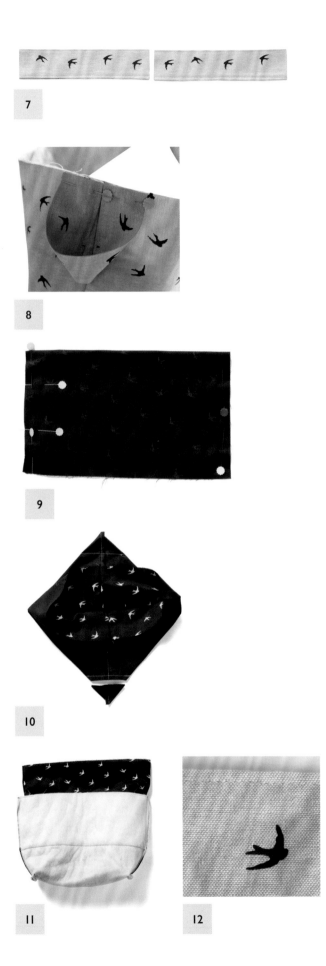

7

8

9

10

11

12

LARGE BASKET YOU'LL NEED:

FABRIC

Requirements based on fabrics with a useable width of 107cm (42in):

- 20in (50cm) dark blue fabric for the outer base and lining

- 10in (25cm) light blue fabric for the outer basket and handles

WADDING (BATTING)

- 12½ × 18in (31.5cm × 45.7cm) fusible wadding (batting)

HABERDASHERY

- Dark blue thread

- Light blue thread

CUTTING (LARGE BASKET)

All cutting instructions include a 0.65cm (¼in) seam allowance.

Dark blue fabric

- One 12½ × 9in (31.5 × 22.9cm) rectangle

- One 12½ × 17½in (31.5 × 47cm) rectangle

Light blue fabric

- Two 12½ × 5in (31.5 × 12.7cm) rectangles

- One 3½ × 13½in (8.9 × 34.2cm) strip

To stitch the large storage basket, follow the instructions for the small basket but substitute the fabrics for those listed above. In Steps 4 and 10 increase the measurement for shaping the base to 1½in (4cm).

TABLE RUNNER

This runner is perfect for creating a focal point on a table of any size. The fabric choices in my table runner are inspired by summer, however you could easily substitute them for a winter or Christmas theme or use a minimalistic colour palette to suit your décor.

SKILL LEVEL: EASY

YOU'LL NEED:

FABRIC

Requirements based on fabrics with a useable width of 107cm (42in):

- 25in (63.5cm) blue fabric for the patchwork, borders and binding

- 10in (25cm) gold fabric for the patchwork

- 4in (10cm) pink fabric for the patchwork

- 15in (38cm) grey fabric for the backing

WADDING (BATTING)

- 15 x 42in (38 x 107cm) wadding (batting)

HABERDASHERY

- Marking pencil

- Neutral thread for piecing

- Dark beige thread for quilting

Tip

When sewing the border strips to the patchwork, stitch the seam with the patchwork facing upwards. This way you can see where the seams intersect and so are less likely to lose any points in the seam line.

TABLE RUNNER

Size: 14 x 41in (35.8 x 104cm)

PREPARATION

The centre of the runner is made up of six repeating blocks. The blocks are then surrounded by a border and quilted.

> *Tip*
>
> To quilt the diagonal lines across the table runner, use the diagonal seam lines as guide and stitch ½in (1.3cm) away from these seam lines.

CUTTING

All cutting instructions include a ¼in (0.65cm) seam allowance.

Blue fabric

- Twelve 3⅞in (9.8cm) squares
- Two 2¾ x 36½in (7 x 92.7cm) strips
- Two 2¾ x 14in (7 x 35.8cm) strips
- Three 2in (5cm) x width of fabric strips

Gold fabric

- Eighteen 3⅞in (9.8cm) squares

Pink fabric

- Six 3⅞in (9.8cm) squares

METHOD

To stitch the patchwork:

1 Draw a line on the wrong side of the gold squares from corner to corner. Place twelve of the gold squares on top of the blue squares, right sides together. Pin, then stitch a scant ¼in (0.65cm) away from each side of the drawn line, then cut along this line. Press seams towards the blue fabric. Trim points.

2 Repeat Step 1 with the remaining six gold squares and the six pink squares. Press seams towards the pink fabric. Trim points.

3 Stitch the units completed in Steps 1 and 2 together into twelve rows of three units. Each row should have blue/gold, pink/gold, blue/gold half-square triangle units. Use the image for placement and correct orientation. Press all seams in the same direction.

4 To stitch one block, take two of the units completed in Step 3 and turn one unit upside down so that the pink triangle in the middle is facing the opposite way. Stitch the units together, matching seams. Press seams downwards.

5 Repeat Step 4 with the remaining units until six blocks are completed. Stitch the blocks together in a line. Press seams downwards.

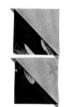

1

2

3

4

5

To add the border:

6 To add the outer border, stitch a 2¾ × 36½in (7 × 92.7cm) blue strip to each side of the unit completed in Step 5. Press seams towards the strip. Then stitch a 2¾ × 14in (7 × 35.8cm) blue strip to each end of the unit. Press seams towards the strip.

To finish the table runner:

7 Layer the table runner by placing the 15 × 42in (38 × 107cm) rectangle of grey backing fabric wrong side up on a surface, followed by the wadding (batting) and then the table runner top, positioned in the centre and right side up. Secure the quilt sandwich with tacking (basting) stitches or quilters' pins placed at regular intervals. The wadding (batting) and backing will be slightly larger than the patchwork top. The table runner is machine quilted with a dark beige thread in diagonal lines 4½in (11.5cm) apart across the runner. When the quilting is completed, trim the excess backing and wadding (batting) level with the edge of the table runner.

8 Stitch the three 2in (5cm) × width of fabric blue strips together to form one continuous strip. Press seams open to reduce bulk. Fold the strip in half lengthwise, wrong sides together, and press. Match the raw edges of the binding to the raw edges of the table runner and sew in place. Fold the binding over to the back of the runner and neatly slip stitch in place by hand.

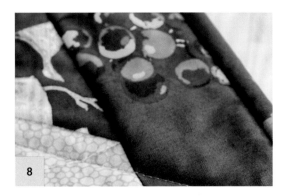

TABLE SET

These handy placemats and coasters are ever so practical as they are washable and handy for protecting your table. I have made mine as a set of two, but it is easy to make more if you are entertaining a crowd.

SKILL LEVEL: EASY

YOU'LL NEED:

FABRIC

Requirements based on fabrics with a useable width of 107cm (42in):

- 20in (50cm) blue fabric for the patchwork, background and binding and for the backing on the coasters

- 3in (7.5cm) gold fabric for the patchwork

- 15in (38cm) grey fabric for the placemat backing

WADDING (BATTING)

- 15in (38cm) wadding (batting)

HABERDASHERY

- 5in (12.7cm) medium weight fusible interfacing
- Neutral thread for piecing
- Navy thread for quilting

Tips

If you are using a big scale directional print for the placemats take time to check that the print is correctly orientated when you get to Step 4.

If you require the coaster inner to be more substantial you could choose to use a thicker interfacing or alternatively a heat resistant wadding (batting).

TABLE SET

. . . .

Size:
Placemats 16½ x 12½in (42 x 31.7cm)

Coasters 4in (10cm) square

PREPARATION:

. . . .

The fabric requirements allow for two
placemats and two matching coasters.
Each placemat contains four small
triangle units, while the coasters
feature one.

CUTTING (FOR TWO PLACEMATS)

. . . .

All cutting instructions include
a ¼in (0.65cm) seam allowance.

Blue fabric

- Two 2½ x 12½in (5 x 31.7cm) strips

- Two 12½in (31.7cm) squares

- Four 2⅞in (7.3cm) squares

- Four 2½in (6.3cm) squares

- Four 2in (5cm) x width of fabric strips

Gold fabric

- Four 2⅞in (7.3cm) squares

Grey fabric

- Two 16½ x 12½in
  (42 x 31.7cm) rectangles

Wadding (batting)

- Two 16½ x 12½in
  (42 x 31.7cm) rectangles

CUTTING (FOR TWO COASTERS)

All cutting instructions include a ¼in (0.65cm) seam allowance.

Blue fabric

- One 2⅞in (7.3cm) square

- Two 1½ x 2½in (4 x 5cm) strips

- Four 1½ x 3½in (4 x 8.9cm) strips

- Two 1½ x 4½in (4 x 11.5cm) strips

- Two 4½in (11.5cm) squares

Gold fabric

- One 2⅞in (7.3cm) square

Fusible interfacing

- Two 4½in (11.5cm) squares

METHOD

To stitch the patchwork for the placemats:

1 Draw a line on the wrong side of the gold squares from corner to corner. Place the gold squares on top of the 2⅞in (7.3cm) blue squares, right sides together. Pin, then stitch a scant ¼in (0.65cm) away from each side of the drawn line and cut along this line. Press seams towards the blue fabric. Trim points. Lay out four units in a row, stitch together and press seams one way. Repeat with the remaining four half-square triangles to create a second row.

To stitch the placemats together:

2 Stitch a 2½in (6.3cm) blue square to both ends of each row. Press seams towards the blue squares.

3 Stitch a 2 x 12½in (5 x 31.7cm) blue strip to the right-hand side of the row and a 12½in (31.7cm) blue square to the left-hand side.
Press seams away from the patchwork.

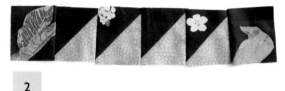

To finish the placemats:

4 Layer each of the placemats ready for quilting by placing the 16½ x 12½in (42 x 31.7cm) rectangle of grey backing fabric wrong side up on a surface, followed by the wadding (batting) and then the placemat top right side up. Secure the quilt sandwich with tacking (basting) stitches or quilters' pins placed at regular intervals. Using navy thread, machine quilt vertical lines 2in (5cm) apart across each placemat.

5 Stitch the four blue 2in (5cm) x width of fabric strips together to form one continuous strip. Press seams open to reduce bulk. Fold the strip in half lengthwise, wrong sides together, and press. Match the raw edges of the binding to the raw edges of the placemats and sew in place. Fold the binding over to the back of the placemat and neatly slip stitch in place by hand.

5

To stitch the patchwork for the coasters:

6 Follow the instructions in Step 1 for the placemats but use one gold and one blue square.

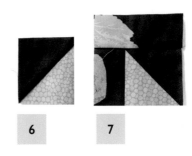

6   7

To stitch the coasters together:

7 Stitch a 1½ x 2in (4 x 5cm) blue strip to one side each of the half-square triangles. Press seam away from the centre.

8 Turn the unit one quarter turn and stitch a 1½ x 3½in (4 x 8.9cm) blue strip to the second side. Press seam away from the centre.

9 Stitch the 1½ x 3½in (4 x 8.9cm) blue strip to the third side and finally sew the 1½ x 4½in (4 x 11.5cm) blue strip to the fourth side, pressing seams away from the centre.

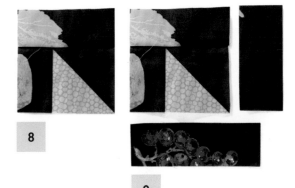

8

9

To finish the coasters:

10 Iron a 4½in (11.5cm) square of interfacing to the wrong side of each unit. Place the units on top of the 4½in (11.5cm) blue squares, right sides together. Stitch around each side, leaving a 1½in (4cm) gap in stitching. Trim corners and turn through. Press carefully. Topstitch around the outer edge ⅛in (0.32cm) away from the edge, closing the opening in the side as you go. Using the navy thread quilt ¼in (0.65cm) away from the outer edge of each triangle.

10

TEA COSY

Keep your teapot warm and toasty with this beautiful cosy. Not only will it help keep the tea hot, but it will brighten up your kitchen at the same time. I have made mine to match the Table Runner and Table Set to give a coordinated feel to my home.

SKILL LEVEL: EASY

YOU'LL NEED:

FABRIC

Requirements based on fabrics with a useable width of 107cm (42in):

- 15in (38cm) blue fabric for the patchwork and tea cosy outer

- 3in (7.5cm) gold fabric for the patchwork

- 12in (33cm) grey fabric for the lining

WADDING (BATTING)

- 12in (33cm) fusible wadding (batting)

HABERDASHERY

- Marking pencil

- Neutral thread for piecing

- Navy thread for quilting

> **Tip**
>
> This would be a great project to make from fabric scraps. For a totally unique look, each of the sections could be a different fabric.

TEA COSY

Size: 16 × 11½in (40.6 × 29cm)

PREPARATION

The tea cosy has the same design on each side which is made up of six triangle units and is fully lined with a shaped top.

> *Tip*
>
> The cosy is reversible so could be used inside out if required.

CUTTING

All cutting instructions include a ¼in (0.65cm) seam allowance.

Blue fabric

- Two 16½ × 2½in (42 × 5cm) strips
- Two 16½ × 8in (42 × 20.3cm) rectangles
- Six 2⅞in (7.3cm) squares
- Four 2½in (6.3cm) squares

Gold fabric

- Six 2⅞in (7.3cm) squares

Grey fabric

- Two 16½ × 12in (42 × 30cm) rectangles

Fusible wadding (batting)

- Two 16½ × 12in (42 × 30cm) rectangles

METHOD

To stitch the patchwork:

1 Draw a line on the wrong side of the gold squares from corner to corner. Place the gold squares on top of the 2⅞in (7.3cm) blue squares, right sides together. Pin, then stitch a scant ¼in (0.65cm) away from each side of the drawn line. Press seams towards the blue fabric and trim points. Stitch the half-square triangles together into two rows of six units. Press seams one way.

To stitch the tea cosy together:

2 Stitch a 2½in (6.3cm) blue square to each end of the rows completed in Step 1. Press seams towards the blue squares. Then sew a 16½ × 2in (42 × 5cm) blue strip to one side of the row and a 16½ × 8in (42 × 20.3cm) blue rectangle to the other. Press seams away from the patchwork.

3 Iron the fusible wadding (batting) to the wrong side of both of the units. Quilt vertical lines from top to bottom at 2in (5cm) intervals.

4 To shape the top of the tea cosy, take one outer section. Measure 5in (12.7cm) down from the corner on one side and mark this point. Then measure 5in (12.7cm) along the top from the same corner and mark this points. Using a plate or circle template, draw a curve from point to point. Use scissors to cut along the curve. Repeat on the corners of the outer cosy sections and on the two 16½ × 12in (42 × 30cm) grey rectangles for the lining.

1

2

3

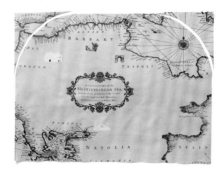

4

5 Place the two outer tea cosy sections right sides together and stitch up each short side and along the curved top. Clip curves. Turn right side out and press.

6 To stitch the inner lining section together, place the two 12 × 16½in (30 × 42cm) grey curved top rectangles right sides together and stitch up each short side and along the curved top, leaving a 4in (10.2cm) gap in stitching in the centre of the top. Clip curves. Place the outer cosy inside the lining, right sides together, and pin all the way around the edge. Stitch together, matching the side seams.

To finish the tea cosy:

7 Turn the tea cosy right side out through the gap and stitch the opening closed.

8 Carefully press the cosy and then topstitch ¼in (0.65cm) away from the bottom outer edge.

5

6

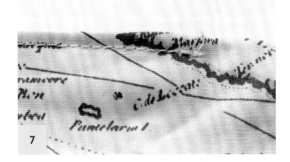
7

8

MARKET TOTE

This large bag has sturdy handles and is strong enough to carry those even heavier items of shopping. It is softly padded with wadding (batting) and has an internal pocket for storing your shopping list or coupons. As soon as your friends see it, they will want you to make them one too!

SKILL LEVEL: EASY

YOU'LL NEED:

FABRIC

Requirements based on fabrics with a useable width of 107cm (42in):

- 40in (1m) green fabric for the outer bag sides, handles, lining and pocket

- 12in (30cm) stripe fabric for the outer bag centres

- 14in (36cm) pink fabric for the outer bag base

WADDING (BATTING)

- 40in (1m) fusible wadding (batting)

HABERDASHERY

- Neutral thread for piecing

- Green thread for quilting

> **Tip**
>
> Avoid using a directional print for the outer bag base (the pink fabric). The fabric wraps around the bottom of the bag which results in the fabric on one side being upside down.

MARKET TOTE

Size: 16½ × 16½ × 4½in (42 × 42 × 11.5cm)

PREPARATION:

The bag is made from three fabrics with the third fabric also being used for the lining. The sides and base are quilted with a wavy pattern to add texture.

Tip

To ensure that the wavy quilted lines are even, place pins at 2½in (6.3cm) intervals down each side and then quilt in-between the pins.

CUTTING

All cutting instructions include a ¼in (0.65cm) seam allowance.

Green fabric

- One 17 × 35in (43.2 × 89cm) rectangle
- One 7 × 17in (17.8 × 43.2cm) rectangle
- Four 5 × 12in (12.7 × 30cm) rectangles
- Two 3½ × 21½in (8.9 × 54.6cm) strips

Stripe fabric

- Two 8 × 12in (20.3 × 30cm) rectangles

Pink fabric

- One 13 × 17in (33 × 43.2cm) rectangle

Fusible wadding (batting)

- One 17 × 36in (43.2 × 91.4cm) rectangle
- Two 1¼ × 21½in (3.2 × 54.6cm) strips

METHOD

To stitch the outer bag and pocket:

1 Stitch a 5 × 12in (12.7 × 30cm) green rectangle to each side of an 8 × 12in (20.3 × 30cm) stripe rectangle. Press seams towards the centre panel. Stitch each of these units to each side of the 13 × 17in (33 × 43.2cm) pink rectangle. Press seams towards the pink rectangle.

2 Iron the 17 × 36in (43.2 × 91.4cm) fusible wadding (batting) rectangle to the reverse of the unit completed in Step 1. Quilt the unit by quilting wavy horizontal lines across the panel at 2½in (6.3cm) intervals using green thread.

To stitch the handles:

3 Take the two 3½ × 21½in (8.9 × 54.6cm) green strips and press under ¼in (0.65cm) on one long edge of each. Lay a 1¼ × 21½in (3.2 × 54.6cm) strip of fusible wadding (batting) along the centre of the wrong side of each green strip and iron in place. Fold the raw edge of the fabric to the centre of the wadding (batting) and then the folded edge on top. The folded edge should overlap the raw edge by ¼in (0.65cm). Pin in place and topstitch along the folded edge. To strengthen the handle, sew ¼in (0.65cm) in from the outer edge on both handles.

4 Place a raw end of one handle level with the raw edge of the outer bag panel completed in Step 2. The centre of the handle should sit over the centre of the seam line where the stripe centre panel meets a green side panel. Repeat with the other end of the handle. Stitch in place with an ⅛in (0.32cm) seam. Repeat with the second handle.

1

2

3

4

To stitch the pocket:

5 Take the 7 × 17in (17.8 × 43.2cm) green rectangle and fold in half right sides together so that the top edge measures 8½in (21.6cm). Stitch around the three edges, leaving a 2in (5cm) gap in stitching in the middle of one short side. Trim the corners, turn right sides out through the gap and press. Position the completed pocket on one short edge of the 17 × 35in (43.2 × 89cm) green rectangle, in the centre and 3in (7.5cm) down from the top. Topstitch down each side and across the bottom leaving the top edge open.

To stitch the bag together:

6 To stitch the lining fold the 17 × 35in (43.2 × 89cm) green rectangle in half, right sides together, and sew down each side, leaving a 4in (10cm) gap in stitching on one side. To shape the base of the lining, match the centre fold of the base with the side seam. Measure in 2½in (6.3cm) along the seam line, draw a line with a pencil and ruler then stitch across.

7 Cut off the excess fabric. Repeat on the other corner.

5

6

7

8 To stitch the outer bag fold the unit completed in Step 4 right sides together and sew down each side, ensuring that the handles are kept out of the way of the stitching. Shape the base of the outer bag by following the instructions in Steps 6 and 7. Turn the outer bag right side out.

To finish the bag:

9 Place the outer bag inside the lining so that the right side of the lining is facing the right side of the bag. Match the side seams and pin to hold in place. Keep the handles pushed down inside the bag. Stitch around the top. Turn the bag through the opening in the lining and stitch the gap in the lining closed. Sew ¼in (0.65cm) around the top edge of the bag.

COIN PURSE

This little purse uses small pieces of fabric and so is perfect for precious scraps. It makes a lovely gift and is robust enough for everyday use. Quick and easy to make, you could make up a batch in a weekend and in a variety of fabrics to match your shopping bags or totes.

SKILL LEVEL: EASY

YOU'LL NEED:

FABRIC

Requirements based on fabrics with a useable width of 107cm (42in):

- 2in (5cm) pale blue for the purse top

- 4in (10cm) pink fabric for the outer purse

- 4in (10cm) green for the lining

HABERDASHERY

- 2in (5cm) diameter circle template (or use an appropriately sized cup)

- 2in (5cm) fusible medium weight interfacing

- 4in (10cm) metal zip

- Neutral thread for piecing

Tips

It can be difficult to find small metal zips that are an exact match to your fabric so choose a zip colour that contrasts and make a feature of it.

A ribbon could be added to the zipper pull but, if you choose to do this, don't make the ribbon too long otherwise it could catch in the zip.

COIN PURSE

Size: 4 × 4 × 5½in (10 × 10 × 14cm)

PREPARATION:

The purse uses three different fabrics and closes with a metal zip. The top band is strengthened by interfacing which helps to hold the shape.

CUTTING

All cutting instructions include a ¼in (0.65cm) seam allowance.

Pale blue fabric

- Four 4½ × 1½in (11.5 × 4cm) strips

Pink fabric

- Two 6½ × 3½in (16.5 × 8.9cm) rectangles

Green fabric

- Two 6½ × 3½in (16.5 × 8.9cm) rectangles

Fusible medium weight interfacing

- Four 4½ × 1½in (11.5 × 4cm) strips

METHOD

To stitch the outer purse and lining:

1 Take two 4½ x 1½in (11.5 x 4cm) pale blue strips and iron the interfacing to the wrong side of each. Next, take the two 6½ x 3½in (16.5 x 8.9cm) pink rectangles and use the circle template to draw a curve on the two bottom corners of each. Cut away the excess fabric. Sew a gathering thread to the top section of both the pink units by increasing the stitch length on your sewing machine to the maximum setting to create a long stitch, then sewing ⅛in (0.32cm) in from the edge of the fabric. Gently pull on the thread to gather the fabric.

2 Stitch a pink unit to a pale blue strip, ensuring that the gathers are equally spaced. Press the seam towards the strip.

3 Repeat Steps 1 and 2 with the remaining two pale blue strips and two 6½ x 3½in (16.5 x 8.9cm) green rectangles.

To stitch the purse together:

4 To attach the zip, place the outer pink purse section on a surface right side up and put the zip face down on front of it, matching the top edge. Place the lining on top, right side down, and stitch along the top edge to secure the lining, zip and outer purse. To attach the zip to the second purse section, repeat as for the first. Open out each panel and press. Stitch and ⅛in (0.32cm) each side of the zip.

To finish the purse:

5 Open the zip halfway and place the two outer purse sections right sides together, and also the lining panels right sides together. Pin then stitch all the way around the edge, leaving a 2in (5cm) gap in stitching in the bottom of the lining. Clip the curved edges. Turn the purse through the opening in the lining and stitch the opening closed. Tuck the lining neatly inside the purse.

1

2

3

4

5

WEEKEND BAG

This large, roomy bag is perfect for storing your travel essentials, from overnight basics to produce from the local shop. The top is finished with a zip so you can keep everything inside secure. The sides are soft and pliable so it can easily be folded when not in use.

SKILL LEVEL: REQUIRES EXPERIENCE

YOU'LL NEED:

FABRIC

Requirements based on fabrics with a useable width of 107cm (42in):

- 15in (38cm) navy birds for the outer bag sides

- 10in (25cm) blue and white wave for the outer bag centres

- 20in (50cm) floral print for the outer bag base and handles

- 40in (1m) blue patterned fabric for the lining

WADDING (BATTING)

- 40in (1m) fusible wadding (batting)

HABERDASHERY

- Neutral thread for piecing
- Dark grey thread for quilting
- 22in (56cm) navy zip

Tip

The fabric requirements allow for directional prints but, before cutting do double-check that you have the fabric design correctly positioned.

WEEKEND BAG

Size: 22 × 16 × 5in (56 × 40.6 × 12.7cm)

PREPARATION

The project uses three fabrics for the outer bag and one for the lining. The quilting adds a softness to the bag.

CUTTING

All cutting instructions include a ¼in (0.65cm) seam allowance.

Navy birds fabric

- Four 7¼ × 13in (18.4 × 33cm) rectangles

Blue and white wave fabric

- Two 9 × 13in (23 × 33cm) rectangles

Floral print fabric

- Two 22½ × 7in (57 × 17.8cm) rectangles

- Two 3 × 60in (7.5 × 152cm) strips (sew together to get the required length)

Blue patterned fabric

- Two 22½ × 19in (57 × 48.3cm) rectangles

Fusible wadding (batting)

- Two 22½ × 19½in (57 × 49.5cm) rectangles

- Two 1 × 60in (2.5 × 152cm) strips (these can be joined together to get the required length)

METHOD

To stitch the outer bag:

1 Stitch a 7¼ × 13in (18.4 × 33cm) navy birds rectangle to each side of a 9 × 13in (23 × 33cm) blue and white wave rectangle. Press seams away from the centre panel. Repeat to make a second unit.

2 Stitch a 22½ × 7in (57 × 17.8cm) floral print rectangle to the bottom of each unit completed in Step 1. Press seams towards the floral print fabric. Iron the 22½ × 19½in (57 × 49.5cm) fusible wadding (batting) rectangles to the reverse of each of the units then quilt them. I used dark grey thread to quilt wavy horizontal lines across the panels at 2in (5cm) intervals.

To stitch the handles:

3 Take the two 3 × 60in (7.5 × 152cm) floral print strips. Fold and press under ¼in (0.65cm) along one long side of each. Lay the 1in (2.5cm) strips of fusible wadding (batting) strips on the wrong edge of the fabric, end to end along the length. The edge of the wadding (batting) should be 1in (2.5cm) away from the raw edge of the fabric. Iron the wadding (batting) strips to fuse in place.

4 Fold the raw edge of the floral print strip on top of the wadding (batting) and then the folded edge on top of this. Pin in place. Using a thread that tones, topstitch along the folded edge.

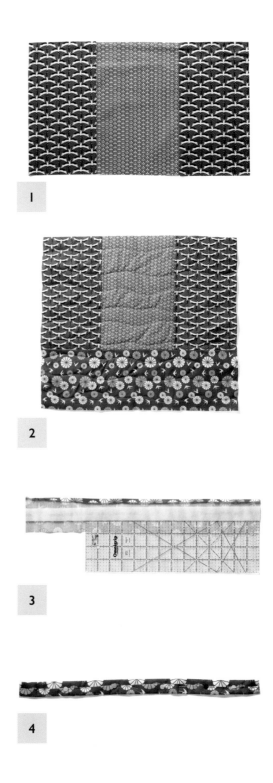

1

2

3

4

5 Take one handle and lay it along the seam between the centre panel and the right-hand section of one of the units completed in Step 2. Make sure it is centred along the seam line and that the raw edge on the bottom of the handle extends ¼in (0.65cm) over the seam line where the base joins the top section of the bag. The folded side of the handle should be right sides together with the outer bag. Pin in place, stopping 3in (7.5cm) from the top of the bag. Align the opposite end of the same handle with the seam line between the centre panel and the left-hand section and pin. Repeat with the other handle. Turn under the bottom ¼in (0.65cm) of each handle and pin or tack (baste) in place. Topstitch along both sides of each handle, across the bottom and across the top at the 3in (7.5cm) marking.

To stitch the bag together:

6 To attach the zip place the first outer bag section right side up and place the zip face down on front of it, matching the top edge. Place the lining on top, right side down, and stitch along the top edge to secure the lining, zip and outer.

Tip

My bag doesn't have internal pockets but if you wish to add them sew them to the lining pieces before starting Step 7.

7 Repeat Step 6 to attach the zip to the second outer bag section, then open out and press. Stitch ¼in (0.65cm) each side of the zip.

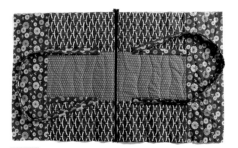

7

8 Open the zip halfway and place the two outer bag sections right sides facing, and the lining panels also rights side facing. Pin and stitch all the way around the edge, leaving a 6in (15.2cm) gap in stitching on one side of the lining.

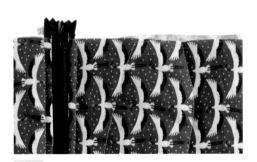

8

To finish the bag:

9 To shape the base, match the centre fold of the base with the side seam. Measure in 2in (5cm) along the seam line and stitch across. Cut off the excess fabric. Repeat on the other corner, and then on both corners of the lining. Turn the bag through the opening in the lining so it is right side out. Stitch the opening closed. Carefully press the lining and outer bag.

9

RESOURCES

Fabrics
Makower *www.makoweruk.com*
Hantex *www.hantex.co.uk*
Higgs and Higgs *www.higgsandhiggs.com*

Fusible wadding (batting)
Plush Addict *www.plushaddict.co.uk*

Wadding (batting)
Lady Sew and Sew
www.ladysewandsew.co.uk

Interfacing
www.vlieseline.com

Thread
Aurifil threads *www.aurifil.com*

Fusible interfacing
Just Between Friends
www.justbetweenfriends.co.uk

Sewing machine
Bernina *www.bernina.com*

ACKNOWLEDGEMENTS

I have so enjoyed designing, creating and writing the patterns for the projects in this book and am very grateful to everyone who played a part in the process. Thanks to Elizabeth Betts for her meticulous technical editing and endless patience. To Makower, Hantex and Higgs & Higgs thank you for all the lovely fabrics to work with. Finally, thank you to my partner Alan who is so supportive with my fabric obsession.

Janet Goddard

INDEX

To order a book, or to request
a catalogue, contact:

GMC Publications Ltd
Castle Place, 166 High Street,
Lewes, East Sussex,
BN7 1XU
United Kingdom
Tel: +44 (0)1273 488005
www.gmcbooks.com